Smart
in
India

Eat Smart in India

How to Decipher the Menu
Know the Market Foods
&
Embark on a Tasting Adventure

Joan Peterson and Indu Menon

Illustrated by Susan Chwae

GINKGO PRESS™ INC

Madison, Wisconsin

Eat Smart in India

Joan B. Peterson and Indu Menon

Map lettering is by Gail L. Carlson; cover and insert photographs are by Joan Peterson; author photographs are by Susan Chwae.

The quote by James A. Michener from "This Great Big Wonderful World," from the March 1956 issue of Travel-Holiday Magazine, © 1956 by James A. Michener, is reprinted by permission of the William Morris Agency, Inc. on behalf of the author.

Publisher's Cataloging-in-Publication

(Provided by Quality Books, Inc.)

Peterson, Joan (Joan B.)

Eat smart in India : how to decipher the menu, know the market foods & embark on a tasting adventure / Joan Peterson and Indu Menon; illustrated by Susan Chwae.

p. cm.

Includes bibliographical references and index.

Preassigned Control Number: 2003109140

ISBN 0-9641168-7-1

1. Cookery, Indic. 2. Diet--India. 3. Food habits--India. 4. Cookery--India. 5. India--Guidebooks. I. Menon, Indu, 1963- II. Title.

TX724.5.I4P38 2004 641.5954

QBI03-200376

Printed in the United States of America

To J. Inder Singh (Jiggs) Kalra

His love and knowledge of Indian food
added savor to every page.

Contents

Preface

> If you reject the food, ignore the customs, fear the religion and avoid the people, you might better stay home. You are like a pebble thrown into water; you become wet on the surface but you are never a part of the water.
>
> —James A. Michener

There is no more satisfying way to get immersed in a new culture than to mingle with local people in the places where they enjoy good food and conversation—in their favorite neighborhood cafés, restaurants, picnic spots or outdoor markets. I try to capture the essence of a country through its food, and seek out unfamiliar ingredients and preparations that provide new tastes. By meandering on foot or navigating on local buses, I have discovered serendipitously many memorable eateries away from more heavily trafficked tourist areas. As an unexpected but cherished diner, I have had the pleasure of seeing my efforts in learning the cuisine appreciated by the people in ways that make an understanding of each other's language unimportant.

Each trip energizes me as though it were my first; the preparation for a visit becomes about as exciting as the trip itself. Once I determine the destination, I begin to accumulate information—buying relevant guidebooks, raiding the libraries and sifting through my hefty collection of travel articles and clippings for useful data. A high priority for me is the creation of a reference list of the foods, with translations, from my resource materials. For all but a few popular European destinations, however, the amount of information devoted to food is limited. General travel guides and phrase books contain only an overview of the cuisine because they cover so many other subjects of interest to travelers. Not surprisingly, the reference lists I compiled from these sources were inadequate; too many items on menus were unrecognizable. Some menus have translations but these often are more amusing than helpful, and waiters usually cannot provide further assistance in interpreting them. Furthermore, small neighborhood establishments—some of my favorite dining spots—frequently lack menus and post their daily offerings, typically in the native language, on chalkboards outside the door. So unless you are adequately familiar with food words, you may pass up good tasting experiences!

To make dining a more satisfying cultural experience for myself and for others, I resolved on an earlier vacation to improve upon the reference lists I always compiled and research the food "on the spot" throughout my next trip. Upon my return, I would generate a comprehensive guidebook, making it easier for future travelers to know the cuisine. The book that resulted from that "next trip" featured the cuisine of Brazil and represented the first in what would be a series of in-depth explorations of the foods of foreign countries; to date six other EAT SMART guides have been published. These cover the cuisines of Turkey, Indonesia, Mexico, Poland, Morocco and India. My intention is to enable the traveler to decipher the menu with confidence and shop or browse in supermarkets and fascinating, lively outdoor food and spice markets empowered with greater knowledge.

I am pleased to introduce Indu Menon, co-author of this book. Indu was born in India but has lived in Canada and the United States for much of her life. Her extensive knowledge of the rich culinary heritage of her native country has been invaluable to this project.

Indu and I had many memorable culinary experiences while traveling around India. One such experience that greatly enhanced our trip occurred on a hunting estate, Chhatra Sagar, near the village of Nimaj in the state of Rajasthan. We stayed a few days with Man Singh Rathore and his wife, Durga Kanware, and their family, who offer guests both Rajput hospitality in a unique setting and the opportunity to learn about traditional Rajasthani cuisine in the family kitchen.

The guest accommodations on the estate are novel and sumptuous. On the terrace-like top of a dam overlooking a natural water reserve is a row of spacious tents, each with modern amenities, fit for royalty. From these tents, one can enjoy breathtaking views of the sunrise and sunset, with the Aravalli Hills in the distance.

Meals are taken *al fresco* in the cooling shade of a nearby master tent. Our hosts, Harshvardhan Singh Rathore (the son of Man Singh Rathore) and his wife, Shri Nidhi, described in detail each dish served, and talked about spices and ingredients used in Rajasthani dishes. Later, we watched the preparation of several dishes during a demonstration with the family cooks. The most intriguing special ingredients are sun-dried or pickled famine-survival foods from the arid regions of Rajasthan. *Kair* is a small, berry-like fruit grown on a leafless, thorny tree. It typically is eaten with two other desert foods: a bean pod (*sangri*) that grows on a different thorny tree and another bean pod called *kumita*. These foods are available when all other vegetation in the Thar desert has dried up. The dish combining them, *kair sangri kumita,* is identified with one of the Rajasthani communities, the Marwari, based around Jodhpur. Despite the importance of these items as survival food during part of the year, they are eaten year round and also enjoyed fresh. Another dish we watched our hosts prepare was *pittore,* a delicious concoction of spicy chickpea-flour "dumplings" in a yogurt-based sauce. Their recipe is included in our guide on p. 51.

Our hosts offer Jeep safari trips in the countryside, so we visited some traditional farms and even sighted a few of the antelope called black bucks (*Antelope cervircapra*). The males have long, spiraled horns that can reach two feet in length. Crops of wheat, chile peppers, mustard and cotton grow on lands irrigated with reservoir water. Much of the land was once owned by our hosts. After India's independence from the British in 1947, lands were redistributed and the farmhands became landowners. It was obvious, however, that the change in ownership did not change the way the people looked up to their former "patrons." We met a shepherd that morning and Harshvardhan called to him to show us what he had for lunch. Wrapped in a cloth sack were two *chappatis* with a layer of red pepper and garlic paste between them. He even offered us a taste!

The purpose of the EAT SMART guides is to encourage sampling new and often unusual foods, and to discover new ways of preparing or combining familiar ingredients. What better way is there to get to know a culture than through its cuisine? We know informed travelers will be more open to experimentation. The EAT SMART guides also will help steer the traveler away from foods they want to avoid—everyone confesses to disliking something!

This guide has four main chapters. The first provides a history of Indian cuisine. It is followed by a chapter with descriptions of regional Indian foods. The other main chapters are extensive listings, placed near the end of the book for easy reference. The *Menu Guide* is an alphabetical compilation of menu entries, including general Indian fare as well as regional specialties. Some not-to-be-missed dishes with country-wide popularity are labeled "national favorite" in the margin next to the menu entry. Some classic regional dishes of India—also not to be missed—are labeled "regional classic." The *Foods & Flavors Guide* contains a translation of food items and terms associated with preparing and serving food. This glossary will be useful in interpreting menus, since it is impractical to cover in the *Menu Guide* all the flavors or combinations possible for certain dishes.

Also included in the book is a chapter offering hints on browsing and shopping in the food markets and one with phrases that will be useful in restaurants and food markets to learn more about the foods of India. A chapter is devoted to classic Indian recipes. Do take time to experiment with these recipes before departure; it is a wonderful and immediately rewarding way to preview Indian food. Most special Indian ingredients in these recipes can be obtained in the United States; substitutions for unavailable ingredients are given. Sources of hard-to-find Indian ingredients can be found in the *Resources* chapter, which also cites groups that focus on travel to India or offer the opportunity to have person-to-person contact through home visits to gain a deeper understanding of the country, including its cuisine.

At the end of the book is a form for ordering additional copies of this book or any of our other EAT SMART guides directly from Ginkgo Press,™ Inc. The back of the form has space for your comments and suggestions. Ginkgo Press would like to hear from you, our readers, about your culinary experiences in India. Your comments and suggestions will be helpful for future editions of this book.

JOAN PETERSON & INDU MENON
Madison, Wisconsin

Acknowledgments

We gratefully acknowledge those who assisted us in preparing this book. Nawab Jafar Mir Abdullah, Veena Arora, Sanjay Bhat, Debasish Guha, Sandeep Kalia, J. Inder Singh (Jiggs) Kalra, Durga Kanwar, Sahebzade Syeda Uzma Khan, Velayudhan Koolichalakal, Vivek Kulkarni, P.K. Vikram Kumar, Indumati Menon, Meenakshi Meyyappan, Shobha Mohan, Sadhana Mukherji, Rajam Nagarajan, Shri Nidhi, Hemant Oberoi, Pushpesh Pant, Alphonso Pereira, Raju P.K., Gulam Rasool, Harshvardhan Singh Rathore, Man Singh Rathore, Cruz Urbano Do Rego, Julia Carmen de Sa, Chaman Lal Sharma, Rajeev Sharma, Sanjeev Sharma, J.P. Singh, Vikramaditya Singh Sodawas, Ananda Solomon, Preeti Vaid, and the culinary staff of Spice Coast Cruises for contributing recipes from their private collections (regretably, some could not be used because of space limitations); Susan Chwae (Ginkgo Press) for her distinctive illustrations, knockout cover design, and classy photographs of the authors; and Nicol Knappen (Ekeby) for bringing the text neatly to order.

We are indebted to many people for introducing us to regional foods, for presenting cooking demonstrations, for help in identifying regional Indian foods and menu items, for reading the manuscript, for providing resource materials, or for guide and touring services. Thanks to M.G.K. and Indumati Menon; Preeti Vaid; Farzana Contractor (editor/publisher, *Upper Crust,* Mumbai, Maharashtra); Rati Godrej; Jonathan M. Kenoyer, field director of the Harappa Archaeological Research Project; Jeannette Belliveau, Beau Monde Books; C.R. ("Skip") Johnson; Anand and Tejal Gokhani; Premila Dias Fernandes (Institute of Hotel Management, Goa); Chef Fernando (owner, Fernando's Nostalgia Restaurant, Goa); Dharmendra Kanwar; Air Chief Marshall and Mrs. Bilkees Latif; Maya Nagin; Anita Pottekat; Maria Celeste Fernandes; Versha Sirohi; Kamal Rawat (The Claridges, New Delhi);

Deep Raj (Laxmi Vilas Palace, Bharatpur, Rajasthan); Biju Mathew (co-owner, Karakkattil House Spice Plantation, Kumily, Kerala); Geeta Bhatnagar; A.S. Qureshi and Mayank Bali (master chef and senior chef de partie, respectively, Masala Art of Taj Palace, New Delhi); Mir Sheik Ahmadd (owner, Nayaab Restaurant, Hyderabad, Andhra Pradesh); J.P. Singh and Madhulika Bhattacharya (chef and events/communications manager, respectively, Bukhara Restaurant, ITC Maurya Sheraton, New Delhi); Sanjeev Sharma, Vimal Seth, and Alpana Singh (executive assistant manager, general manager and sales manager, respectively, Taj Residency, Lucknow, Uttar Pradesh); Jayaram Banan (owner, Sagar Restaurant, New Delhi); Debasish Guha and Santanu Bhattacharya (sous chef and food/beverage manager, respectively, Aaheli Restaurant, Peerless Inn, Kolkata, West Bengal); Ved Prakash Pardal (owner, Niros Restaurant, Jaipur, Rajasthan); Chaman Lal Sharma and Lata Murkot Ramunny (senior sous chef and sales manager, respectively, Taj Banjara, Hyderabad, Andhra Pradesh); Sunitha Divakaran N. and Erine Louis (junior sous chef and manager, respectively, The Brunton Boatyard, Fort Cochin, Kerala); Rajeev Sharma (executive chef, Hotel Samode Palace, Samode, Rajasthan); Vikramaditya Singh Sodawas (Karni Group of Hotels, Jodhpur, Rajasthan); Rakhi Dasgupta (owner/chef of Kewpies Restaurant, Kolkata, West Bengal); Sangeeta Bhatnagar; R.K. Saxena (director, Institute of Hotel Management, Lucknow, Uttar Pradesh); P.K. Vikram Kumar and Prakash Menon (chef and general manager, respectively, Taj Garden Retreat, Madurai, Tamil Nadu); Mumtaz Khan (owner/teacher, Cooking Classes and Catering, Hyderabad, Andhra Pradesh); Pradeep Khosla (executive chef, Taj Bengal, Kolkata, West Bengal); Ravi Kothari (general manager, Four Seasons Vegetarian Restaurant, Jaipur, Rajasthan); Ved Lal Pandita (executive manager, Chor Bizarre, Hotel Broadway, Delhi); Pobre Pereira (Martins Corner, Goa); Dolly Roy (owner, Dolly's, The Tea Shop, Kolkata, West Bengal); Raminder Malhotra and Kamal Makkar (chef and owner, respectively, MerCurries, New Delhi); C.P. and Faiza Moosa (owners/chefs of Ayesha Manzil, Tellicherry, Kerala); M.A. Rasheed (executive chef, Taj Malabar, Cochin, Kerala); Vikas Milhoutra and Digvijay Singh (chef and resident manager, respectively, The Rambagh Palace, Jaipur, Rajasthan); Ragu P.K. and Subrahmanian P. (chef and general manager, respectively, Coconut Lagoon, Kumarakom, Kerala); Ratna Sen (president, Suruchi, the All-Bengal Women's Union Restaurant, Kolkata, West Bengal); Jose Varkey P., Jose Dominic and Doland Alwyn (corporate chef, co-owner and project manager, respectively, Casino Group of Hotels,

Cochin, Kerala); V.K. Prasad (food and beverage manager, Taj Connemara, Chennai, Tamil Nadu); Prawal Potnis (owner, Highway Gomantek, Mumbai, Maharashtra); Sudipto Bhattacharya (sous chef, Park Royal Inter-Continental, New Delhi); Khanraj Joshua (owner, VJ's Home Diner, Chennai, Tamil Nadu); Anil Kumar C. (general manager, Spice Village, Thekkady, Kerala); Veena Arora (chef, Spice Route Restaurant, Imperial Hotel, New Delhi); Sanjay Bhat (chef/manager, Surabhi Restaurant, Jaipur, Rajasthan); Sandeep Kalia (executive chef, Taj Hari Mahal, Jodhpur, Rajasthan); J. Inder Singh (Jiggs) Kalra; Man Singh Rathore, Durga Kanwar, Harshvardhan Singh Rathore and Shri Nidhi (owners, Chhatra Sagar, Nimaj, Rajasthan); the family of Nawab Jafar Mir Abdullah: Sahebzade Syeda Uzma Khan, Begum Almas Abdullah, Begum Iffat Sultan and Begum Ibrahim Ali Khan; Velayudhan Koolichalakal (chef, Spice Village, Casino Group of Hotels, Kerala), Vivek Kulkarni (chef, Taj Mahal, Mumbai, Maharastra); Meenakshi Meyyappan (The Bangala, Karaikudi, Chettinad, Tamil Nadu); Sadhana Mukherji (cookbook author, Kolkata, West Bengal); Alphonso Pereira (executive chef, The Mandovi, Panjim, Goa); Gulam Rasool (chef, Ondhyana, Taj Residency, Lucknow, Uttar Pradesh); Cruz Urbano Do Rego (executive chef, Taj Holiday Village, Goa); Julia Carmen de Sa (executive chef, Taj Exotica, Goa); Ananda Solomon (chef, Konkan Café, President Hotel, Mumbai, Maharashtra) and the culinary staff of Spice Coast Cruises; Prateek Hira and Earl Figg (Tornos Tourist Agency, Lucknow, Uttar Pradesh); Joseph John (manager, Garuda India Holidays, Hyderabad, Andhra Pradesh); Zubin N. Jogina (Jogina Tours, Agra, Uttar Pradesh); P.S. Manoj Kumar, Radha Krishnan and Sayed Rafi (Shree Meenakshi Tours & Travels, Chennai, Tamil Nadu); Surendra S. Rathore, Kuldeep Singh and Bharat Singh (Travel Plan, Jaipur, Rajasthan); Suvendu Mukherjee; Suresh Singh Tanwar (owner, Super Sonic Travels, Mumbai, Maharashtra); J.M. Nirmala Vijayasingh; Sonali Sahgao (International Travel Department, Taj Mumbai, Maharashtra); Savior Cyril and Devi Sundararaj; Alamelu Vairavan and K.M. Mathew.

It is satisfying to note that the executive chefs of many hotel restaurants strive to keep regional Indian cuisine alive, and we especially commend those at the Taj family of business, resort and palace hotels for their efforts in showcasing regional dishes.

We gratefully acknowledge the expert assistance we received from P.N. Narayanaswamy (Mohan) and Shoba Mohan, owners of Travel Scope, New Delhi, for pulling together an itinerary that fulfilled all of our needs perfectly.

They gave generously of their time and also invited us into their home for a feast of southern Indian food. While Indu and I were writing this guide, we had many occasions to ask Mohan for additional background information, and always had what we needed in less than a day. This level of attentiveness to clients is a rarity, and therefore especially appreciated. Travel Scope unquestionably should be anyone's first choice when seeking assistance from a travel agency in planning a trip to India.

Thanks also to Norman and Audrey Stahl, whose unofficial newspaper clipping services kept us well-supplied with timely articles about India.

And special thanks to Brook Soltvedt, a most perceptive and helpful editor.

Eat Smart
in
India

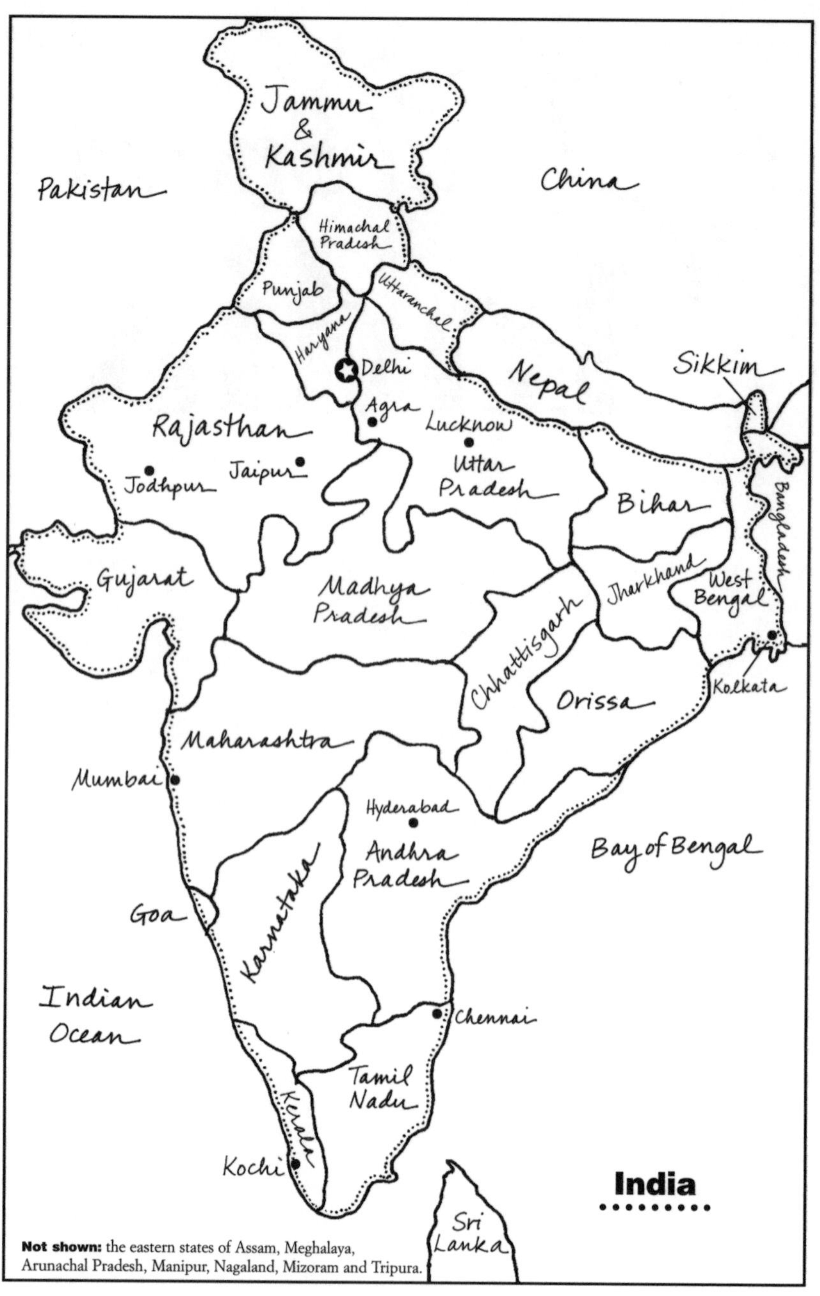

Not shown: the eastern states of Assam, Meghalaya, Arunachal Pradesh, Manipur, Nagaland, Mizoram and Tripura.

The Cuisine of India

An Historical Survey

The vast subcontinent of India has a long, rich history of diverse civilizations. Artifacts found in many ancient settlements chronicle her pre-history and reflect the evolution of early human life from small groups of nomadic hunters and food collectors to advanced agricultural communities providing stable food supplies through plant cultivation and animal domestication.

The transition from hunter to farmer is marked by the presence of Neolithic (New Stone Age) tools dating back to about 5000 BCE. Finely flaked, small stone tools associated with this period have been unearthed in several archeological sites in the Indus Valley in northwestern India, including what is now Pakistan. Also found in the excavations were animal bones and carbonized grains, indicating that the diet of these early cultivators included wheat and barley, and later, oats. Grain was harvested with small, stone blades, stored in pottery jars and processed with primitive querns (grinding stones). Meat and milk were provided by sheep, goats and cattle.

An invaluable, pictorial representation of the prehistoric shift from hunting to farming is portrayed in hundreds of caves comprising the recently discovered (1958) Bhimbetka rock shelter near modern-day Bhopal in the state of Madhya Pradesh. Rock paintings depict everyday scenes beginning about 8000 BCE and ending during Medieval times.

Indus Valley Civilization

India's oldest major civilization was discovered by surprise in 1856. Even the earliest of ancient writings did not hint of its existence. Excavation of the sites commenced in the 1920s with the ancient city of Harappa. The civilization apparently evolved from an earlier, Neolithic society in the Indus Valley and

Impression in clay made by a soapstone seal, found in the excavated site of Mohenjo-daro. It depicts a magnificent humped bull beneath undeciphered Indus symbols, and was used as an identification tag by merchants to indicate ownership of goods.

flourished around 2500 BCE. At this time, hundreds of settlements were located in the plains, the arid highlands and the lowlands along the mighty Indus River and its tributaries. Owing to frequent flooding, deposits of alluvial silt from the riverbed continually re-fertilized the lowland soil and produced prime farmland.

This ancient urban civilization, called the Indus Valley civilization, or the Harappan civilization, was spread over a roughly triangular area about 1,000 miles on each side, covering an area of about 420,000 square miles. It was considerably larger than the earliest-known civilizations of Egypt and Mesopotamia. The two greatest urban centers, Harappa and Mohenjo-daro, each with about 40,000 citizens at its zenith, were almost 400 miles apart. Sites have been excavated as far west as the Arabian seacoast in Baluchistan, Pakistan, to east of Delhi in the state of Uttar Pradesh, to the Himalayas and northern Afghanistan, to the state of Gujarat in the south and Mumbai (Bombay) in the state of Maharashtra.

The inhabitants of the Indus Valley shared a remarkable cultural uniformity. Their well-planned cities and villages were built alike according to the same rectangular patterns. Identical-sized, kiln-fired mud bricks were used to construct houses, and in the larger cities, they were used to erect elaborate, multi-chambered granaries. The people used two standardized series of graded cubic weights made of polished stones based on the weight of a seed called *rati* (the rosary pea, *Abrus precatorius*). To this day, goldsmiths use this same system to weigh gold and diamonds. Potters fashioned uniform styles of wheel-thrown pots. Stone workers produced standardized tools. Artists crafted ornaments and square stamp seals made of soapstone engraved with identical scenes and unique script, which is still undeciphered.

The economy was based on agriculture and animal husbandry. Farmers cultivated wheat, barley, oats, millet, sorghum, rice, peas, chickpeas, lentils, sesame, mustard, figs, dates, grapes, mangoes, pomegranates and melons. Cloth woven of spun cotton was an important trading commodity within the Indus Valley and in Mesopotamia, far beyond. Domesticated goats, sheep, water buffalo and cattle, including the Indian humped cattle (zebu), provided milk, meat and labor. The diet was supplemented with turtles, fish, shellfish and game.

Cooks in early kitchens used several methods to process foods. They husked their grain with a mortar and pestle, and ground it into flour with a quern. They knew how to steam, grill, fry, bake and boil food in water, and had a large variety of clay or metal cooking vessels. It is likely that they made breads such as *chappatis* and *parathas* because many flat pans similar to the *tava,* which is used to cook these breads today, were found at excavation sites. Dairy workers made yogurt and butter from milk. Others made alcoholic beverages in stills made from clay.

The fate of the Indus Valley civilization is unclear. A theory long held by many archeologists—that invaders known as Aryans came from Afghanistan and Central Asia around 1500 BCE and drove out the inhabitants of the Indus Valley—is becoming untenable in light of new evidence found in excavations. Re-interpretations of earlier findings suggest it is more likely that the decline of the Indus Valley civilization, which occurred around 1700 BCE, was attributable to a combination of natural disasters. Persistent flooding of certain rivers and the desertification of others made it necessary for the people to abandon the major urban Indus sites and seek more suitable lands to sustain them.

The Aryans (Vedic Culture)

While the origin of the Aryan people in India remains an evolving study, their culture and literary skills are known in some detail. The Aryans practiced a polytheistic religion called Vedism. They spoke an ancient Sanskrit language

Wheel-thrown, disposable clay drinking cups called "pointed-base goblets," found at Harappa. The grooves may have been decorative or functional, by providing a firmer grip. Original images courtesy of the Harappa Archaeology Research Project.

and wrote four lengthy volumes of scriptures known as the Vedas—the *Rig Veda, Sama Veda, Yajur Veda* and *Atharva Veda*—which are a collection of hymns, incantations and rituals. The earliest text, the *Rig Veda,* was composed about 1500 BCE and written down about 600 BCE. The Vedas are the oldest recorded history of India, and played a crucial role in the rise of Hinduism and the caste system, in which the status and occupation of a person are determined by birth. Current thought is that these texts may well be much older than the dates accorded them.

The Vedas also recorded every day life in India beginning about four thousand years ago. The Vedic Aryan agriculturalists were said to inhabit lands along the banks of the Saraswati and Drishadvati rivers (both now dry), east of the region that had been home to the Harappan civilization. From their literary works, we learn that they grew barley, wheat, millet, chickpeas, kidney beans, peas, several types of lentils, safflower, mustard, linseed, sesame, garlic, and spices such as turmeric, fenugreek and ginger. They enjoyed fruits, including the pomegranate, jujube, bael (a fruit of the citrus family), Indian gooseberry, orange, lemon, lime and star apple. In the rainy season Aryan farmers grew rice. They planted pumpkins and gourds along riverbanks, just as farmers do today. Visitors to the magnificent Taj Mahal in Agra, who look out at the river behind it, can see such gardens along the riverbanks. Grapes, sugar cane, vegetables, root crops and greens were grown in moist, lowland plots. Aquatic plants such as the lotus were especially prized; both stem and roots are delicious.

Several beverages are mentioned in the Veda texts. Milk was important and came primarily from cattle. Refreshing juices were made from a variety of fruits, especially mango, star apple and grapes. Alcoholic drinks were distilled from honey, grains, fruits, certain flowers and raw sugar. Perhaps the most interesting drink was *soma,* a non-alcoholic, hallucinogenic brew made by crushing the *soma* plant in water, and then straining the juice obtained. The specific plant used to make *soma* has yet to be identified with certainty, but the fly agaric mushroom (*Amanita muscarita*) is a likely candidate. Vedic priests (Brahmins) drank *soma* and offered it to the gods during their rituals. *Soma* juice was also mixed with milk, or combined with yogurt and rice.

The meat-eating Vedic Aryans ate a formidable selection of domestic and wild animals, and had elaborate rites for sacrificing them for food. Taking the life of an animal for this purpose, however, gradually became repugnant, and prohibitions against eating meat under certain conditions began to appear in the literature. For example, it became forbidden to kill cattle that were fecund or lactating, or those that were needed for plowing fields or pulling heavy loads. Finally, killing them under any circumstance was prohibited. Vegetarianism began to emerge and become widespread.

Some culinary preparations described in the Vedas have recognizable modern counterparts. Sweet cakes called *apupa* made of barley or rice flour, fried in clarified butter (*ghee*) and coated with honey compare with the Bengali sweet known as *malpua,* which is made of milk and all-purpose flour, fried in clarified butter and soaked in sugar syrup. A fried cake called *vataka* made from ground lentils corresponds to the southern Indian specialty *vada,* a deep-fried, doughnut-shaped cake also made of ground lentils.

The last Vedic text, the *Atharva Veda,* established a holistic, natural medical system called Ayurveda, which held that wellness is a harmonious balance between the body, mind and spirit. Healing sickness (imbalance) includes a dietary regimen based on two properties of food thought to be therapeutic, taste and temperature, and is dependent on an individual's constitutional type. Meals require all six tastes (*rasas*)—sweet, sour, bitter, salty, pungent and astringent—in the proper proportion, because each taste can modify the body's system to restore balance. Meals also need an equivalent amount of heat- and cold-inducing foods to prevent excessive body warming, believed to cause illness. Ayurveda is still practiced today. For example, yogurt is eaten at the end of a meal to counter the "heat" of the meal.

Two epic poems that were composed around 400 BCE, the *Ramayana* and *Mahabbharata,* reveal that the Aryans began moving east toward the Gangetic basin and southward. Their culture, religious dogmas and food habits ultimately spread all over India.

Buddhism and Jainism

The humanitarian religious movements of Buddhism and Jainism arose around 500 BCE as offshoots of Hinduism. Both began as a reaction to Hindu doctrines and as an effort to reform them. Their founders were not Brahmins (the priest caste), but Kshatriyas (the ruler/warrior caste). They questioned the teachings of the Vedas and the Vedic rites, challenged the caste system and, of special interest here, influenced the eating habits of their followers.

The founder of Buddhism, Siddhartha Gautama (563–483 BCE), was called Buddha (the enlightened one). As a young man he renounced his family and princely station, and for several years adopted an ascetic life of wandering, meditation, and religious austerity. Failing, however, to reach his goal of enlightenment and wisdom through austerity, he turned to advocating a harmonious way of life that struck a balance between self-indulgence and abstinence, and taught non-violence as a way of life.

Buddhists were vegetarians and typically begged for food as an act of humility. They were expected to eat whatever alms were offered. Even meat or fish was permissible if three conditions were met to render these foods "blameless": the recipients had not seen, heard or suspected that an animal had been killed on their behalf. Buddha advised eating grain foods (rice, barley, and wheat), legumes (*urad dal, masoor dal,* mung beans), eggs, honey, clarified butter and sesame seed oil, and enjoined his Buddhist monks to limit their food intake to the hours between sunrise and noon to curb the passions and strengthen the spirit. Several foods not mentioned in earlier literature are listed around 400 BC in Buddhist and Jain texts. The coconut, banana, jackfruit, palm, yam and elephant yam are on the menu at this time, as are the bottle gourd and spinach. Wet rice cultivation was widespread.

The oldest written account of the teachings of Buddha is found in the edicts of Ashoka (268–232 BCE), the greatest of Mauryan kings, who converted to Buddhism after being deeply troubled by the cruelties of war that he had inflicted. The Mauryan Empire (322–185 BCE), with its efficient, centralized administration, for the first time united much of India under one dynasty. It included all of northern India and much of central and southern India. Under Ashoka, Buddhism reached its purest form. His edicts, carved on stone pillars throughout the Empire, explained Buddhism to his subjects, and were instrumental in the successful spread of the religion within and beyond India. Ashoka became a strict vegetarian, made it unlawful to kill animals for food, shunned all violence, including the death penalty, and advocated religious tolerance. His many reforms had a far-reaching effect on Indian culture. While Buddhism is widespread in the world today, it is not practiced to any great extent in India. It was snuffed out as an organized religion by Muslim invaders in the early 1200s.

Jainism was founded by Vardhamana Jnatriputra (540–468 BCE), who, like Buddha, was born into the Kshatriya caste and walked away from a comfortable life to seek salvation. He was called the great hero (Mahavira) and the conquerer (Jina) because he mastered human desire. He and his followers, known as Jains, preached a strict doctrine of non-violence, believing that all life was sacred. They were strict vegetarians, and the food they ate was subject to rigid restrictions to avoid injury to life. Permissible foods were those that would not kill the plant or animal from which it had been taken, such as fruit, nuts and milk. Honey was forbidden because its removal kills the bees. Beverages had to be strained through cloth, and water had to be boiled and strained before drinking. For fear of breathing in living things or squashing them underfoot, Jains wore masks over their mouth and nose, and swept the ground with a broom before walking or sleeping on it. They even eschewed vocations or activities such as agriculture and animal husbandry because they took life. Jainism is still practiced today. In India there are about 5 million adherents, mainly in the area around Mumbai in the western state of Maharashtra.

The Muslims

The Islamization of India took several centuries. At the end of the 600s, Arabs began to launch raids on Sindh, now the southernmost province of Pakistan. This was a time of relative stability in India. The Imperial Gupta dynasty, founded by Chandragupta II in 319 and patterned after the Mauryan Empire, had ended, and a loose federation of kingdoms existed. Society was predominantly Hindu. By the early 700s, Arabs captured Sindh, but further advancement of Muslims into northern India would wait another 300 years.

Elsewhere in the subcontinent in the early 700s a Muslim presence was also beginning to be felt. While Arab spice merchants had been trading in spices and coconut along the Malabar coast (the southern part of India's western coast) for centuries before the birth of the Prophet, many of those arriving in the early 700s had recently converted to Islam. Intermarriage with local women was not uncommon, and the wives converted to Islam. The Mopillah community in northern Kerala became a strong Muslim enclave in this way.

Beginning in 1000, Seljuk Turks from modern Afghanistan, led by Mahmud of Ghazi, swept down the Khyber pass and made the first of what would be many plundering raids by Islamic marauders into the Hindu temple cities of northern India. The Punjab came under Muslim control. In 1192, Arabs led by Mohammed of Ghor, also Seljuk Turks, devastated northern India and by 1202 most of the Hindu kingdoms along the Ganges were annexed to the new Islamic state. Buddhism was exterminated. The Delhi Sultanate was formed in 1206 to bring Muslim territories into political unity.

A notable contribution to Indian cuisine from the Muslims was a variety of flatbreads. These included *naan,* flatbread cooked in a *tandoori,* or clay, oven, *paratha,* griddle-cooked, triangular-shaped, multi-layered flatbread made of wheat flour and clarified butter, and *luchi,* puffy, deep-fried bread made of wheat flour and clarified butter.

The Delhi Sultanate fell in 1526 to Moghuls (Mongols) led by Timur-born Zahir-ud-din Muhammad (Babar), an Islamized descendent of both Genghis Khan and Tamerlane, who had conquered central Asia and Afghanistan before setting his sights on India. Moghul rule ultimately was expanded to include most of the subcontinent, extending as far south as the Krishna River, which flows southeast through the states of Maharashtra, Karnataka and Andhra Pradesh to the Bay of Bengal, subjugating the Hindu majority. As the Moghul Empire, which was ruled from Delhi, began to decline, nobles governing in provincial centers such as Awadh (Lucknow) and Hyderabad established new hereditary kingdoms of Moghul culture. The last Moghul ruler in Delhi was deposed in 1858 by the British.

Lavish architecture and art characterized the Moghul empire in India. The best known example is the glorious and peerless monument—the Taj Mahal—built by Shah Jahan to honor his favorite wife, Mumtaz Mahal. Also lavish was the opulent Moghlai court cuisine, which became assimilated into the Indian menu. Meat (beef, mutton and chicken) was a cherished food, often mixed with fruits and nuts in the Persian tradition, and cooked in rich, creamy sauces. Fragile pieces of hand-pounded edible silver foil decorated many dishes. Elaborate, layered dishes of meat and saffron-flavored rice, called *biryani,* were cooked in lidded pots tightly sealed with a putty-like strip of dough so the pot's contents could slowly steam in its own juices. This characteristically Moghlai style of cooking is called *dumpukht.* Spiced meats were mixed with wheat to make the porridge-like *haleem.* Pastries called *samosas* were stuffed with spicy minced meat or vegetables. The menu of sweets was enhanced by additions such as the frozen dessert called *kulfi. Kulfi* traditionally contained reduced, concentrated milk (*khoya*), sugar, ground pistachios and almonds, with subtle flavoring of saffron, cardamom or rosewater. Deep-fried sweets called *jalebi* were soaked in saffron-flavored sugar syrup. They were made from a batter of flour and yogurt, which was piped in pencil-thin strands onto hot oil in a pattern of loops resembling a row of linked pretzels. *Halva* was made from a variety of mixtures, including lentils, grains, seeds, vegetables and fruits.

The Europeans

The Europeans began to establish trade links in India in the late 15th century. The decline of Moghul power, fueled by dynastic conflicts, opened the way for European intervention. The Portuguese came first (1498), followed by the Dutch (1601), the British (1608) and the French (1719), all aspiring to become rich from the spice trade. While the Portuguese arrived first and left last, it was the British who eclipsed their European maritime rivals and ultimately absorbed the country into the British Empire. India gained her independence from Britain in 1947 after more than 300 years of British dominance, and at the same time was traumatically partitioned along religious lines to create the separate nations of India, with a majority of Hindus, and the predominantly Muslim nations of Pakistan and Bangladesh (then East Pakistan).

The Portuguese

The Portuguese under Vasco da Gama landed on the coast of modern-day Kerala at Kozhikode (Calicut) in 1498. They were the first to establish a sea-route to the fabled riches of the Orient from Europe via the Cape of Good Hope. They took command of the highly profitable spice trade after overpowering Arab merchant seamen, who had enjoyed a trading monopoly for centuries. A trading station was erected in Kochi (Cochin) near the southern tip of Kerala in 1503. Goa, on the western coast, was captured in 1510 and became the hub of the Portuguese empire in India, the Estado da India. In the 1530s, the number of Portuguese enclaves grew to include the island of Diu (within the borders of the state of Gujarat) and the western ports of Mumbai (Bombay), Bassein (near Mumbai) and Daman (Gujarat). On the eastern coast of India, the Portuguese took possession of San Thome near Chennai (Madras) and Hooghly in today's West Bengal. The Portuguese were zealous Catholic missionaries, and the local women they married converted to Catholicism.

In addition to trading in lucrative spices, Portuguese entrepreneurs marketed locally produced commodities such as textiles, especially cotton, and built warehouses to collect and store goods to be loaded onto the ships. The Portuguese enjoyed a monopoly over Indian and Far Eastern trade to Europe for about a century before their influence waned due to lack of sufficient resources to maintain a worldwide empire. In 1961, Indian forces wrested the last of their territories from Portugal, ending a presence in India that had spanned about 450 years.

Illustration of Vasco da Gama, the 6th Portuguese Viceroy of India, in a 17th century history book, from *The Cooking of India* by Santha Rama Rau.

Indian food habits were greatly influenced by the Portuguese. These adventurous seamen were skilled mariners who had founded many overseas settlements in their pursuit of spices. Foods they brought to India came not only from Portugal, but from these colonies. The native names of some of the new foods became incorporated into the Indian lexicon. From Brazil came the cashew nut (*kaju*) and the cashew fruit (actually a pseudo fruit formed from the swollen flower stem), the pineapple (*ananas*) and cassava. From Mexico came corn, cacao and the chile pepper. The New World's bounty also included pork, passion fruit, papaya (*papita*), guava, peanut and sapota (*chickoo*), a fruit with milky latex called chicle, which was used to make chewing gum.

Portuguese influence was the strongest in the Goan Christian community. A characteristic Portuguese dish called *bacalhau,* made with salted, dried codfish, is a well-established favorite. Vinegary preparations are made with meat and seafood. The classic *vindaloo,* a hot-and-sour curry with vinegar, uses a modification of the Portuguese meat, fish or seafood marinade called *vinha de alho,* which consists of vinegar, crushed garlic and seasonings. Goan sausage called *chouriço* was named for the Portuguese version, but is much spicier and made with vinegar instead of wine. In Bengal, the Portuguese introduced the technique of making cheese by acidifying milk. Fresh cheese made this way (*chana* in Bengali; *paneer* in Hindi) is used to create a wide range of famous Bengali sweets. Prior to the arrival of the Portuguese, Bengali sweets were likely to have been made with lentils or milk reduced to a solid by boiling (*khoya*).

The Dutch

The Dutch East India Company (Vereenigde Oostindische Compagnie or VOC) was created in 1602 to contest the Portuguese monopoly of the spice trade. The Dutch (operating under a different shipping company before the VOC was formed) attempted several times to set up a trading station in Surat in present day Gujarat on the western coast of India, beginning in 1601, but they were continually thwarted by the Portuguese, who enjoyed supremacy in the area. The Dutch ceased operations in Gujarat in 1615, only to resume again under better conditions in 1617. In 1607, the Dutch had established enclaves on the Coromandel coast on the southeastern coast of India where they began to monopolize the market. The Dutch gained a toehold in Bengal in 1627. In the 1660s, they seized the Portuguese enclave at Kochi (Cochin) near the southern tip of Kerala and became the undisputed power of the Malabar coast. The Dutch presence in India lasted for about two centuries. They were the most powerful European player in India for more than half of this time. Their commercial operations essentially ended at the close of the 18th century, and by 1825 they had ceded what remained of their interests in

India to the British. This left the contest for supremacy in India to the two remaining major European powers: the British and French.

Despite their many years in India, the Dutch had little impact on the country. Their foremost objective was business, not colonization or conversion.

The British

Anxious to challenge Portuguese and Dutch control of the highly profitable spice trade, a London trading company—the East India Company—was granted a charter from Queen Elizabeth I in 1600, giving it a monopoly on British trade with India. The company established a presence in 1612 at the western port of Surat in Gujarat after receiving a concession to establish the trading station from the ruling Moghul emperor, Jahangir. In 1640 the company leased land in Chennai (Madras). Mumbai (Bombay) was transferred from the Portuguese to the British in 1668 as part of the dowry of Catherine of Braganza of Portugal when she married King Charles II of England, and in 1690 the company established an enclave in Kolkata (Calcutta) in present-day West Bengal on the Hooghly River.

Spices were not the only commodities that proved profitable to market in Europe. The East India Company created high demand for indigo, a dye for uniforms; saltpeter, used for gunpowder; and Indian textiles such as silk, cotton, chintz, brocades, calico, taffetas and muslin.

The East India Company ultimately gained control of trade in India over its European rivals in 1769, partly through clever alliances with local rulers and partly through success on the battlefield. By this time, the company had transformed from a consortium of traders to political leaders who were increasingly involved with local affairs. The company administered the country under an organizational system called the Raj. In 1858, following several lengthy revolts against the British in various parts of the subcontinent, the British Royal Crown seized control of its interests in India from the company and assumed authority over what it termed its "Jewel in the Crown." While India remained a cluster of states, the hegemony of the British Raj gradually increased until the native rulers of most of these principalities, the Hindu maharajas and Muslim nawabs, were only nominally independent.

Attempts to address the concerns of colonial exploitation of India and the discrimination against her citizens by the British escalated in the late 19th century. In 1885 the Indian National Congress was formed. It became the means for the rise of Indian nationalism and the push for self-rule. Led by Mohandas Karamchand (Mahatma) Gandhi, India achieved independence non-violently in 1947, but at great cost. With about 15 percent of the population, the Muslim minority was wary of an independent India led by Hindus. Through the Muslim League, they insisted that India be partitioned into Muslim and Hindu states. The Muslim states of Pakistan and Bangladesh were formed, and massive upheaval and violence ensued as Hindus left these areas and Muslims moved to them.

The British influence on Indian food habits was minimal, despite more than 300 years of dominance on the subcontinent. Rather, the opposite occurred: Indian food became deeply rooted in English cuisine. Perhaps the greatest British contribution to the Indian larder was tea. Although tea plants were discovered in the state of Assam in the 1820s, it wasn't until 1830, when the Chinese tea trade with England came to a standstill, that the British considered cultivating tea in India. Since plants brought from China did not thrive well, the commercial venture began with the indigenous plants. The plantations growing Assam and Darjeeling tea were enormously successful. Both varieties were named after the places where they were grown. Darjeeling was a British hill station and elite resort in the present day state of West Bengal.

The British put their stamp on a handful of Indian dishes. For example, the British were accustomed to having soup as the starter course of a meal. Not only were Indian meals served without courses, anything resembling a soup was a thin sauce eaten along with everything else in the meal. In an

Nutmeg and mace, coveted spice treasures of the Orient. Nutmeg is within the seed shell. Mace is the lacy seed covering.

attempt to maintain some aspect of their culinary traditions, the British in India created a soup called *mulligatawny,* using a corruption of the Tamil (a southern Indian language) words *milagu* and *tunni* meaning "pepper water." The soup was concocted from meat stock and chunks of meat flavored with onion, garlic, chile pepper, coriander, cumin and fenugreek. The British added fish to the classic dish of lentils, rice and spices, known to Indians as *khichri*. The dish was renamed *kedgeree* and demoted to the status of a leftover. In Bengal, two misused English words became part of the culinary lexicon. A "chop" referred to a stuffed potato pancake dipped in egg and bread crumbs and fried. A "cutlet" was similarly coated and fried, but consisted of shrimp or meat pounded flat, with the tail or piece of bone still attached. The British perpetrated a misconception about Indian food when they popularized the word curry. *Kari,* the source word for curry, is Tamil for black pepper. Indians associated *kari* with a dish of vegetables with spices, and later, a sauce or gravy. By extension, it came to mean a dish with sauce or gravy. Unfortunately, in British usage, "curry" became synonymous with Indian food, and implied a standard powdered mixture of spices sold in packets to achieve the Indian curry taste. Indians, however, use freshly ground spices, and no such standardized mixture for a curry exists in their kitchens.

The French

In 1664, the French East India Company (Compagnie des Indes Orientales) was chartered by King Louis XIV to mount a serious challenge to the trading successes of Britain and the Netherlands. It was not until 1719 that the company became established in India. The hub of the French settlements was Pondicherry, located on the Coromandel coast of present day Tamil Nadu. Other enclaves of French imperial ambition were established at Karikal (also on the Coromandel coast of the state of Tamil Nadu), Mahe (on the Malabar coast of Kerala), Surat (Gujarat) and the inland trade settlement of Chandernagore (also known as Chandarnagar, in present-day West Bengal).

By the end of the 17th century, the English East India Company had outmaneuvered the Dutch and Portuguese, and the French thus were the only serious competition facing them. Under Joseph François Dupleix, the French began an aggressive policy of expansion to secure political authority and trade supremacy in southern India. The French and British fought three bitter wars, called the Carnatic Wars, between 1746 and 1763. The British under Robert Clive ultimately were victorious. Lacking sufficient funds to maintain its operations, the French East India Company folded in 1769. The trading stations of Pondicherry and Chandernagore remained under French control until they were formally transferred to India in 1962.

French culinary influence in India essentially was contained in Pondicherry. The baguette and croissant, pâtés, spicy pork sausages such as *boudin,* croquettes of minced fish or meat, sponge cakes and crème caramel custard are legacies of the French in Pondicherry.

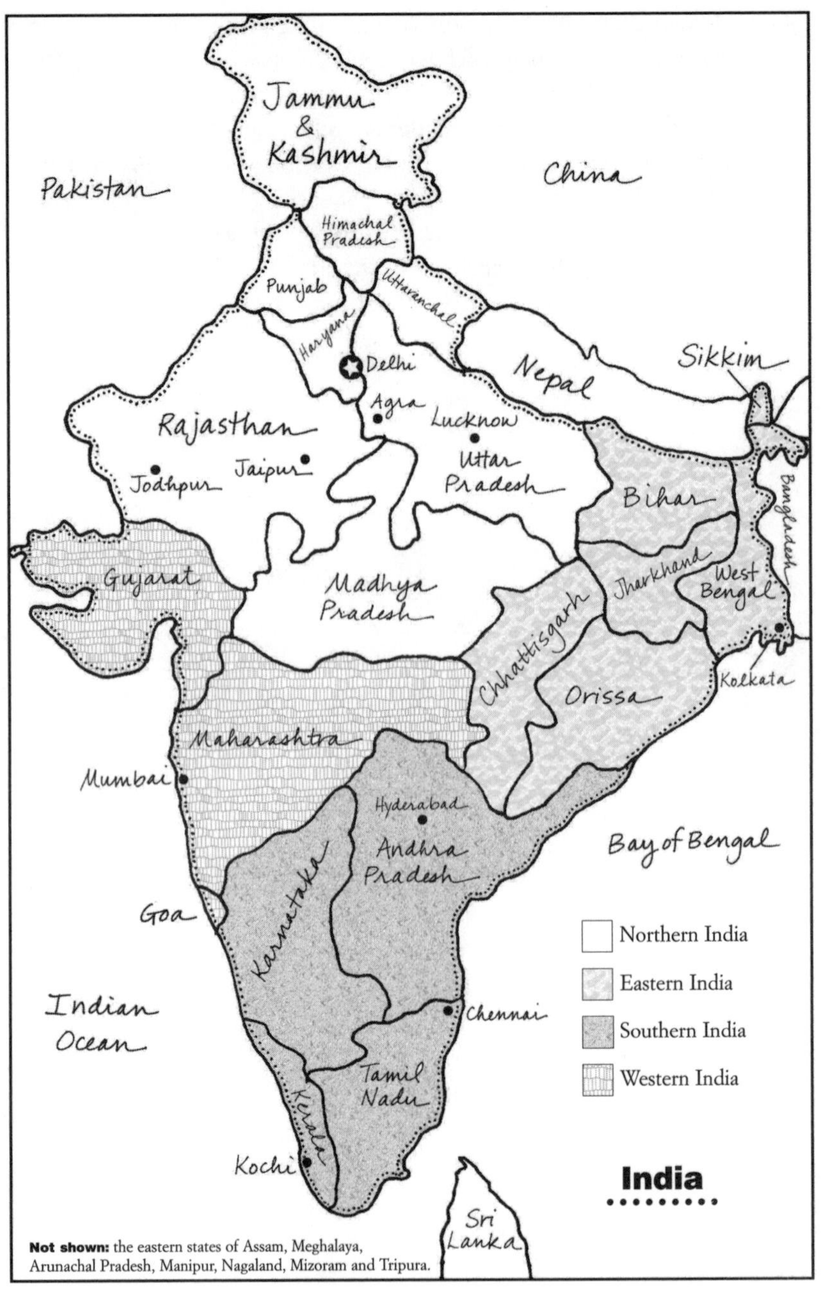

Not shown: the eastern states of Assam, Meghalaya, Arunachal Pradesh, Manipur, Nagaland, Mizoram and Tripura.

Regional Indian Food

A Quick Tour of Indian Foods and Their Regional Variations

Indian Food in a Nutshell

Spices and herbs are the cornerstone of Indian cookery. Traditionally they are freshly ground twice a day in a shallow stone mortar or on a flat basalt stone using a basalt rolling pin. Chefs and home cooks alike are well versed in the individual characteristics of each seasoning. They know which spices enhance the flavors of particular foods, how much of each spice should be added to a dish, and in what order spices should be added in the cooking process so that no spice predominates or tastes "raw." Artful blending of different seasonings has created the subtle nuances in the characteristic tastes of Indian cuisine.

In general, spice mixtures (*masalas*) are either wet or dry. Wet mixtures are moistened with water, oil, vinegar or coconut milk to make a paste or more liquid mixture, and they cannot be stored. Dry mixtures mainly are powdered. In Indian cooking there is no all-purpose curry powder. This is a commercial mixture created during colonial times by the British, who still use it rather indiscriminately to make "Indian" dishes. To an Indian, a curry (*kari*) is a sauce, or a dish with sauce.

Wet mixtures of fresh spices predominate in southern Indian cooking. Here the main staple is rice, and although it typically is boiled and eaten plain, several flavored sauces accompany the rice to moisten it. In northern Indian cooking, many dishes tend to be cooked without much liquid, and as such are easier to scoop up with pieces of bread as a utensil. Without sauce to cook in, spices are tempered in a small amount of clarified butter or oil to release their aromas before the main ingredients are added to the pan. In some recipes, tempered spices are added at the end of the cooking process.

Spices are grouped by their cooling or warming effects on the body. Each group of spices is stored separately in a spice box (*masala dabba*), a round stainless steel box holding several round, open metal containers. A plate fits tightly between the box lid and the individual containers so that the spices do not mix or lose their aroma. Some spices having a warming effect include ginger, cumin, ajwain seeds, black cardamom, cinnamon, mace, nutmeg, turmeric and red and green chile peppers. Spices having a cooling effect include anise, fennel, basil, green cardamom, cilantro and mint. Special regional spice mixtures will be described in the appropriate regional section.

Indians favor the visual appeal of certain spices. Turmeric gives a bright yellow color to rice and potatoes. The very expensive saffron lends an orange-yellow color besides its incomparable, heady flavor. Mild red chile peppers grown in Kashmir are prized for the rich red color they impart. Another red colorant, an edible extract called *mowal,* is made by boiling cockscomb flowers. Dried rind of the red mango (*kokum*) turns food somewhat pinkish-purple. We especially like the refreshing, slightly tart drink (*kokum kadi*) of fresh coconut milk flavored with this rind.

Among the unusual spices to experience is asafoetida (*hing*), a strong, sulfur-smelling, milky gum resin. A pinch of powdered resin cooked in hot oil or clarified butter and added to certain dishes enhances the flavor. A trace of the odor component of the resin lasts for a short while in the food. Curry leaves (*kari patta*) are small, dark-green leaves with a distinct aroma and slightly bitter taste. They are are sizzled in a little clarified butter or oil to accentuate their flavor. Fenugreek leaves (*kasoori methi*) have a unique, slightly bitter flavor. It is an acquired taste, which can be sampled in *aloo methi,* diced potatoes fried with fresh fenugreek leaves. Bits of dried fenugreek leaves occasionally are added to flatbread dough. *Kewra* essence is extracted from the flowers of the screwpine and is used in rice- or corn-flour noodles called *falooda.* These flavored noodles are an ingredient in a drink, which is also called *falooda,* and they accompany Indian ice cream made with reduced milk. Certain lichens are used as herbs. *Kalpasi* is a lichen that grows on cinnamon trees and on trees near the seashore during the monsoon.

Several kinds of salt are used in Indian dishes. Some are flavored salts mined as crystals from underground dry sea beds. Each imparts a characteristic flavor based on its chemical composition. For example, black mineral salt (*kala namak*) adds zest to snacks (*chaat*), fruit salads and vegetables. Its grayish-pink crystals become grayish-brown when ground.

Masala dabba, the traditional stainless steel spice box found in almost every Indian kitchen. The spices in their individual containers are kept fresh and unmixed by a tight-fitting plate that sits atop the spice containers. The *masala dabba* also includes a lid and small teaspoon.

A variety of souring agents add piquancy to Indian dishes. Vinegar, lemon juice, tamarind water and yogurt are more common. Fresh or dried pomegranate seeds, powdered dried mango, dried rind of the red mango (*kokum*), citric acid powder and powdered dried *kachri,* a short little cucumber, are also used.

Indians sweeten their food with unprocessed sugar made in villages from sugar cane juice or palm juice. The juices are boiled to a thick syrup, which is cooled and solidified in molds of various shapes for sale in the markets. This product, *jaggery* or *gur,* has a special, rich caramel-like flavor that is superior to brown sugar. Granulated sugar is also widely used as a sweetener.

Unlike Westerners, who serve meals in courses, Indians serve all dishes at once. Food is placed in serving bowls on the table or ladled into small matching metal bowls placed around the edge of a shallow-rimmed, round metal plate. *Thali* refers to this serving plate and to a meal served in this style. Rice (or bread in some regions) is served in the center of the plate. In southern India, a banana leaf replaces the metal thali for special occasions, and food is placed directly on the leaf. Traditionally, food is eaten by hand (the right hand, that is) with or without a "utensil" made of bread. Try eating some meals without cutlery. Before long it will seem natural.

What Indians eat at mealtime depends on many factors. Although weather and geography play a major role in food and eating habits, so do religious and caste restrictions. India is home to a profusion of faiths. Indians may be Hindus, Muslims, Jains, Sikhs, Christians, Zoroastrians (the Parsis, a sect that emigrated from Persia in 650 to escape religious persecution), Jews (most emigrated to Israel or other countries after World War II) or members of several minor faiths. Many of these groups have food taboos. For example, meat, fowl, fish, shellfish and eggs are forbidden for strict vegetarians (Brahmin Hindus and Jains).

Since India has had a long tradition of vegetarianism and the majority of the people are vegetarians, a discussion of vegetables is a good place to start describing the Indian pantry. A typical meal includes more than one vegetable dish. Vegetables taste delicious in Indian food, no matter how they are cooked. It's uncanny how vegetables you may not have liked taste good in Indian preparations and those you already like taste even better. The two basic cooking methods are dry and wet. The dry method uses no water; vegetables are fried with spices in a little clarified butter. There are several names for this simple way of cooking vegetables, depending on where in the country the dish is made. The wet cooking method yields a gravy or sauce from added water or aromatic broth. Meals usually include a yogurt relish (*raita*) with chopped or grated vegetables. Tasty vegetable fritters with a chickpea batter coating are a popular snack.

Not surprisingly, the outdoor markets spill over with vegetables in great abundance. You may be startled to see that native Indian carrots are black or bright red. They are sweeter than the orange variety. Greens are widely enjoyed, especially mustard greens, white radish greens, fenugreek greens, amaranth and spinach. Some novel vegetables from our perspective are cluster bean (*guar phali*; the source of a gum used as a thickener), elephant-foot yam (*jamikand*), unripe jackfruit, the desert famine food of Rajasthan (*kair, sangri*

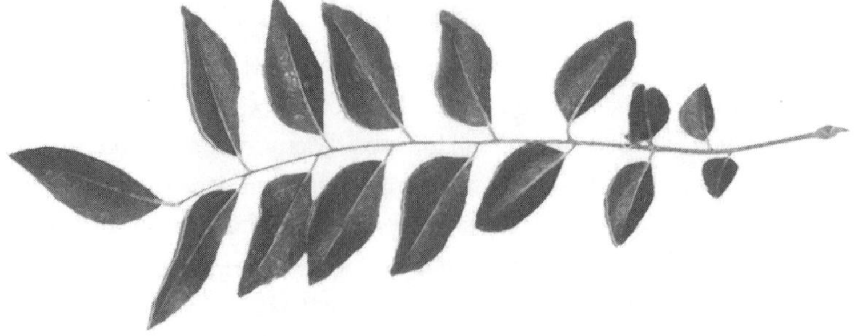

Fresh sprig of fragrant curry leaves. Sizzling the leaves in a little oil accentuates their aroma and slightly bitter taste. This spice provides a signature flavor to southern Indian dishes.

and *kumita*), a bean-like pod called drumstick (*sahan*), a sweet yellow cucumber (*taute*), baby Indian squash (*tinda*) and a variety of gourds: pointed gourd (*parval*), bitter gourd (*karela*), ridged gourd (*ghosala*), bottle gourd (*doodhi*), snake gourd (*chichinda*), ash gourd (*petha*) and a tiny, round gourd called *chundakai.* Lotus root and stem are prized; puffed lotus seeds are eaten on fast days when no grain is eaten.

No meal is complete without a dish of legumes (*dal*). They are an important protein-rich staple food for meatless meals and are enormously versatile. Dal is used to make thick soupy preparations, stews, chutneys, crêpes, steamed cakes, sprouted salads and sweets. *Dal* is available whole or split, with or without skins, oiled or not oiled, and also ground into flour. *Urad dal,* or black gram, is a lentil named for its black seed coat. Without its seed coat, the lentil is cream-colored, usually split, and known in this form as white gram. *Chana dal* is a matte yellow variety of chickpea usually sold split. It is also known as Bengal gram, attesting to its popularity in eastern India. *Chana dal* is ground into flour called *besan,* which is used to make dumplings and batter coatings. *Masoor dal* is a split red lentil. The yellow *moong dal* is a split mung bean. Whole mung beans have a green skin and sometimes are called green gram.

Grains play a critical role in the diet. All meals include rice or bread. Rice is an important grain throughout India, but more so in southern and eastern India, where it is the predominant grain, usually eaten twice a day. Many types of long- and short-grained rice are cultivated in the country; each region grows its own variety, largely for local consumption. Unquestionably, the most prized is the aromatic long-grained *basmati* rice, aged to intensify its flavor. It is showcased in elegant rice pilafs and elaborate steamed rice and meat (or vegetable) dishes known as *biryani.* Rice is also ground to make flour, pounded into flakes and puffed.

Wheat is the major grain in northern India, and is most often used to make traditional unleavened flatbreads. These mouth-watering breads are cooked or fried on a griddle, or baked in a clay oven (*tandoor*), and eaten while still warm. Simple griddle-cooked breads made only of flour and water are the so-called daily breads. Oil or clarified butter, even milk, sometimes is added to tenderize the dough. Daily breads include *chappati* (*roti*) and *phulka,* which is like a *chappati* but puffed by holding an undercooked side over an open flame. *Paratha,* also a daily bread, is griddle-fried in a little clarified butter. It is triangular and multi-layered, and it can also be stuffed. When *paratha* is stuffed, typically with potato or other vegetables, it often is round to make it easier to fill. On holidays or festive occasions, look for the deep-fried *puri.* It puffs up like a balloon when fried, a process hastened by spooning hot oil over the dough. *Naan,* baked in a clay oven, is a teardrop-shaped leavened flatbread made with white flour. The dough is enriched with yogurt, eggs and clarified butter. The Europeans (Portuguese, Dutch, British and French) introduced yeast during colonial days. Loaves of European-style bread leavened with yeast became known as *dubble roti.* Regional breadstuffs are made with flour ground from millet, sorghum, rice, chickpeas and corn.

Milk is a vital source of protein in the vegetarian diet and is used to make butter, clarified butter (*ghee*), cream, yogurt, reduced milk (*khoya*) and farmer's cheese (*paneer*). Urban dwellers buy cow's milk from government-run dairies. In rural areas of the north, buffalo milk is fairly common since families maintain buffalo for use in the fields. Cow and buffalo milk is much preferred over that from goats and sheep. Milk is sweetened and drunk warm. *Khoya*, sold in markets in blocks like wheels of cheese, is used to make ice cream and a wide variety of sweets. *Paneer* (*chhana*) is made by curdling boiled milk with vinegar or lemon juice. The white curds are strained to remove the whey and flattened under a weight to draw out excess whey and set the cheese.

Many Indians depend on dietary meat, but meat consumption in India presents many complications because of the variety of religious restrictions. Muslims, Christians, Zoroastrians and Jews make up about twenty percent of the population, and they eat meat daily if they can afford it. Chicken is a great favorite. Typically the meat is cut up into pieces, with the skin removed so it doesn't hinder penetration of spices into the meat. Goat is the most popular red meat. Lamb is favored in cooler parts of the country such as Kashmir, where the climate is more suitable for raising sheep. Oddly enough, in India the meat from both animals is called mutton in English, although in England mutton refers to an older and tougher cut of meat from a sheep, not from a goat. In all likelihood, a traveler to India will eat more meat from goats than from sheep. Muslims and Jews eschew pork and Hindus, Jains and Sikhs are forbidden to eat beef, or indeed, any meat, if they are orthodox vegetarians. Not all Brahmin Hindus are vegetarians. Kashmiri Pandits eat meat other than beef. During religious festivals, Bengali Brahmins eat meat from ritually killed animals (though never cows) because the meat is considered sacred. They also eat fish and shellfish.

Fish and shellfish abound in India. There are over 2500 miles of coastline and countless inland waterways and lakes for indigenous and regional freshwater fish. The estuaries of Bengal are home to two local favorites: *illisher,* the silvery, fatty shad, and *bekti,* a fish with boneless flesh. *Kane,* or ladyfish, is a small, silvery and bony freshwater fish found at the confluence of the Gurpur and Netravathi rivers and the Arabian sea in the coastal city of Mangalore in the western state of Karnataka. *Karimeen* is a silver fish with vertical black stripes found in the brackish backwaters of the southern state of Kerala. Perhaps the most interesting fish is *bomil,* or Bombay duck, a milky-white, translucent fish, abundant in the seas around the seven islands comprising the city of Mumbai (Bombay). Bombay duck got its name because locals said its swimming behavior while seeking food near the surface of the water resembled a diving duck. The fish is most often eaten after it has been sun-dried.

Indians love luscious fruits, enjoying them fresh, dried or in the form of chutneys, jams, spicy pickles and cooling beverages. Fruits also appear in a variety of savory dishes. A favorite is the mango, which was brought to Goa by the Portuguese. The Alphonso mango is the premier variety. In addition to the familiar banana, apple, guava, papaya, pineapple, grape and many types of citrus fruits, India offers many tasty exotic fruits. The delicious mangosteen (*manguskai*) has delicate, white, segmented flesh surrounding a single large seed. Its thick purple rind, however, is extremely bitter. The flesh of the sugar apple (*sitaphal*) is sweet, creamy-white, and segmented. Many of the segments enclose a small dark seed. Try to sample the Indian gooseberry (*amla*), sapota (*chikoo*), star apple (*jamun*) and wood apple (*kaith*) as well.

Salads in Indian cuisine are simple preparations. *Raita* is a salad made with seasoned yogurt and chopped vegetables, raw or cooked. Its cooling, refreshing taste is popular everywhere in India. A sweet *raita* with fruits and nuts is

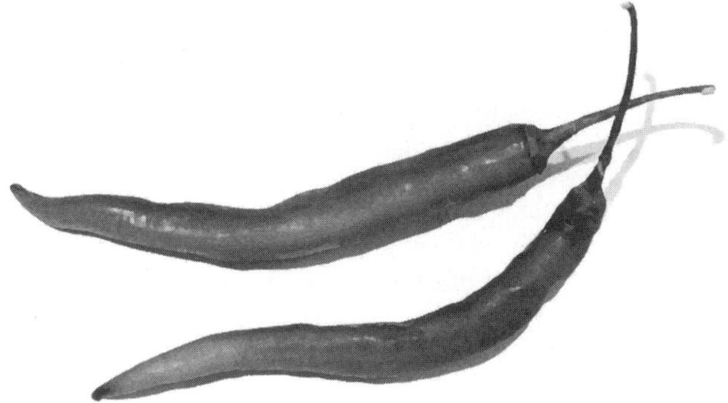

Thin, hot green chile peppers (*hari mirch*) used in vegetable and legume dishes and pickles.

made for special occasions. *Kachumber* is a tangy salad made with a few raw vegetables that are cut up, seasoned and dressed with a little oil or lemon juice. A small portion of a *kachumber* is served on the plate, like a relish.

Pickles and chutneys whet the appetite and accent other dishes. They can be sweet, sour, hot or a combination of tastes, with many regional varieties. A small amount of pickles is an essential part of an Indian meal. Vegetables and fruits are pickled in salt, spices and vinegar or oil, especially mustard oil. Green mango pickle (*aam achar*) is common. Meat, fish and nuts are pickled less commonly. There are many types of pickles and many regional variations. Because pickles keep well, they are a convenience food for travelers and are enjoyed with a variety of flatbreads. A chutney is a pungent relish made from a blend of herbs, spices and a dominant fruit or vegetable. Some chutneys are always served with certain dishes. Lacy crêpes (*dosa*) and steamed "cakes" (*idli*) made from rice and lentils are southern Indian specialties, typically served with fresh coconut chutney.

The daily diet includes salty, spicy, sweet and sour snacks enjoyed anytime between meals. Most are not made at home, but purchased from special snack shops or street vendors. Indians are passionate about simple snacks such as roasted chickpeas and crisps made of chickpea flour, as well as a great variety of complex mixtures. *Bhel puri,* for example, draws raves in Mumbai (Bombay). It contains puffed rice, thin wafers made of lentils, deep-fried vermicelli, potatoes, onions, raw mango and various chutneys. *Pani puri,* another popular snack, begins with small, thin-walled, hollow balls made from rolled circles of bread dough that balloon up when fried in oil. A hole is punched in the top of ball, and the open shell is stuffed with potatoes, bean sprouts and chickpeas, topped with some chutney, and then filled up with spicy cumin and tamarind water. *Pani puri* is best eaten in a single bite to keep the liquid from spilling down your front. Indians always keep some savory snacks such as *chakli* on hand to serve with tea to unexpected visitors. *Chakli* dough, is made of rice flour and chickpea flour dough, is extruded from a press and fried in oil. Delicious!

Sweet tooths take note: every happy occasion is celebrated with sumptuous confections. One category of sweets is made from milk—either milk solids (*khoya*) or soft, unmolded cheese (*chhana*) made from boiled, acidified milk. *Burfi,* a fudge-like tidbit, is one of many made from milk solids and any number of other ingredients. Paper-thin, edible silver foil (*varq*) usually graces the top of each piece of *burfi*. *Kulfi* is a frozen milk-based treat akin to ice cream. It

Kadhai, a two-handled frying and serving pot used to stir fry "dry" dishes and deep fry *puris,* bread rounds of wheat-flour dough that puff up like a balloon in the hot oil.

comes garnished with *falooda,* rice- or corn-flour noodles often flavored with *kewra,* the essence of the screwpine flower. Another irresistible sweet is *gulab jamun,* balls formed from a mixture of milk solids, flour and cardamom. The balls are deep-fried until golden, then soaked in rose- or saffron-flavored sugar syrup. Cheese is the basis of several spectacular concoctions, many of which are creations of Bengali sweetmakers, or *halvais*. *Rossogolla* are spongy white balls made of cheese and flour, which are boiled and served in sugar syrup. Rose essence is added to the syrup when the balls are cool. Sometimes the cheese mixture is tinted with food coloring or formed into different shapes. *Sandesh* is made with a sweetened cheese mixture that is often pressed into molds after it is cooked. *Jalebi* are made by piping a batter of flour and yogurt in pencil-thin strands onto the surface of hot oil in a pattern of loops resembling a row of several pretzels linked together. The loops are then soaked in saffron-flavored sugar syrup. Sweets not based on milk include *halva,* which is made from a variety of mixtures, including lentils, grains, seeds, vegetables and fruits. Milk puddings (*kheer*) and seasonal fresh fruit are typical mealtime sweets.

Undoubtedly, tea is the national beverage. Indians commonly drink it sweetened and mixed with milk and spices (*masala chai*), especially at teatime or at the end of a meal. Sweet or salty chilled yogurt-based drinks (*lassi*) come in a wide assortment of flavors, with mango taking top honors. *Sherbets* are refreshing drinks flavored with fruit juices and syrups, especially rose. Some of our favorites are *jaljeera,* a cumin-flavored, sweet-and-sour cooler with ginger, tamarind, raw sugar and other spices; *sol kadhi,* a cold coconut-milk drink flavored with dried rind of the red mango (*kokum*); and *nimbu pani,* a sweet or salty lime drink. Traditionally, Indians do not drink alcohol at meals, and for a great many, religious restrictions forbid the use of alcohol. There are, however, some intoxicating regional brews, such as the potent liquor called *feni* that is produced in Goa. *Feni* is distilled from palm sap or from the juice of the cashew fruit, a yellow or bright-red pseudo fruit shaped like a bell pepper, from which the cashew nut grows. The cashew trees were brought to Goa by the Portuguese centuries ago.

Betel leaf packets (*paan*), or quids, are chewed at the end of a meal as a digestive aid, stimulant and mouth freshener. The packets have a variety of fillings. Sweet packets (ask for *mitha*) can have some cloves, sugar-coated fennel, cardamom, coconut flakes, rose paste, a bit of tobacco paste, slaked lime and chopped betel nuts. Plain packets (*ask for sada*) lack the sweet components.

The Regions of India

Northern India

The states of Jammu and Kashmir, Punjab, Rajasthan, Himachal Pradesh, Uttar Pradesh, Uttaranchal, Haryana and Madhya Pradesh comprise northern India. The Delhi Union Territory within the state of Uttar Pradesh is a federal

Press used to make *chakli,* a sweet or savory snack made from a dough of rice flour and chick-pea flour. The dough is extruded from the press through the disk with the single star-shaped opening. The extruded, rough-edged cylinder is coiled into a spiral about 2 inches in diameter and then fried.

district containing Delhi, the capital of India. Delhi is divided into two sections: "Old Delhi," the capital of Muslim India for many centuries, and "New Delhi," the imperial city built by the British in the early twentieth century as the nation's capital.

The vast northernmost state has two names, Jammu and Kashmir. The Kashmir region, predominantly Muslim, takes in the lush Kashmir valley, which is rimmed by mountain ranges, including the majestic Himalayas. Jammu, in the foothills in the south, is mainly Hindu. The remote Himalayan kingdom of Ladakh, which is primarily Buddhist, is in the northeastern part of the state.

The cuisine of Jammu and Kashmir varies from region to region. Vegetarians rely on the staples of wheat, legumes and a variety of locally grown sweet rice. Kashmiris are predominantly non-vegetarian. Muslims and Hindus alike eat lamb, goat, chicken and fish. The spices constitute the main difference between their cooking styles. Muslim dishes are flavored with onions and garlic; Hindu dishes are seasoned with asafoetida (*hing*) and powdered ginger, and yogurt is used more often. Some of the better-known meat dishes are *rista* and *rogan josh*. *Rista* has balls of finely pounded lamb cooked in a red sauce colored by an extract of cockscomb flowers and flavored with saffron and deep crimson chile peppers, both esteemed Kashmiri-grown products. *Rogan josh* is a spicy preparation of lamb in yogurt sauce flavored with cinnamon, cardamom, cloves, ginger, fennel and Kashmiri chile peppers. Preparations such as *yakhni pulao,* a dish of lamb or chicken added to rice cooked in meat broth, reflect a strong Mughlai influence, as does the use of nuts and dried fruits in gravied dishes. Breads characteristic of the region are *kulcha,* a flatbread made of kneaded white-flour dough, and *sheermal,* a sweet flatbread basted in a saffron-milk solution. *Hak,* a leafy green vegetable, is eaten daily. Kashmiris also enjoy kohlrabi greens, lotus stem and turnips. At teatime carrot halva is likely to be served along with sweetened green tea. A sumptuous formal banquet (*wazwaan*) with as many as thirty-six different dishes traditionally is served for special ceremonies in Kashmir.

The states of Punjab, Haryana and Himachal Pradesh have similar cooking traditions because the latter two states were carved out of Punjab: Himachal Pradesh in 1966, and Haryana in 2000. The partitioning of India at the time of Independence in 1947 had resulted earlier in the transfer of a large area of Punjab to the new nation of Pakistan. Hindus predominate in Haryana and Himachal Pradesh, Sikhs in Punjab.

Tandoori cooking is a notable Punjabi contribution to Indian cuisine, and a style recognized elsewhere in India and outside the country. Large earthen ovens, half buried in the ground and fired with wood, cook a variety of meats, especially kebabs, fish and several types of flatbreads, including the much relished *naan*. Regional vegetarian favorites are *sarson ka saag,* a dish of mustard greens sautéed with onion and tomato in clarified butter; *rajma,* a dish of spicy red kidney beans cooked in a tomato-based sauce; and *kadhi,* chickpea dumplings in yogurt sauce. Milk products feature prominently. Meals typically include buttermilk and *lassi,* a yogurt-based sweet or salty drink available in many flavors.

The northwestern part of Uttar Pradesh became the state of Uttaranchal in 2000. Both states are dominated by mostly vegetarian Hindus. The sacred Hindu city of Banaras (Varanasi) is in Uttar Pradesh, on the banks of the Ganges. *Aloo Banarasi,* small, whole, fried potatoes in a spicy, yogurt-based gravy with cilantro and tamarind, is one of its specialties. Another is *matar samosa,* a small, conical pastry filled with a spiced mixture of mashed peas. Sweets like *jalebi,* deep-fried pretzel-like loops of dough soaked in saffron-flavored sugar syrup, are popular in Banaras. In Agra, the city of the stately Taj Mahal, the sweet specialty is *petha,* crystallized candy made of ash gourd. The city of Lucknow, the capital of Uttar Pradesh, is associated with mouth-watering, non-vegetarian cookery attributed to the Mughals of Awadh (Lucknow today). Charcoal smoking is central to this Muslim cuisine. For example, *kakori kabab* is a kebab of minced lamb, tenderized with papaya, and flavored with smoke. To get the smoky flavor, the mince is put in a bowl and a well is formed in the middle of it to hold a small dish containing a glowing coal topped with clarified butter. The bowl is covered to trap the smoke and allot it to permeate the meat. Similarly tenderized and smoke-flavored lamb patties are *galawat kebab*. An elegant saffron-flavored rice pilaf called *moti pulao* is garnished with small, deep-fried balls made from a mixture of farmer's cheese, finely ground cashews and corn flour and wrapped in pieces of paper-thin edible silver foil. *Makkhan malai* is a delicious breakfast preparation of frothy cream, flavored with saffron and screwpine, and topped with edible silver leaf.

Much of Rajasthan is arid. The Thar desert, comprising the northwestern third of the state, is a sparsely populated region with an austere climate that has dictated a limited menu. During times of famine, sustenance comes from those few deep-rooted plants that survive when all other vegetation has dried up. A dish made with three desert famine foods is *kair sangri kumita*. It has a small, berry-like fruit (*kair*) from a leafless, thorny tree, a small bean pod (*sangri*) that grows on a different thorny tree and another desert berry (*kumita*). This preparation is identified with the Marwari community based around Jodhpur. The Marwari are strict vegetarians and like a generous helping of chile peppers in their food. Gram flour (*besan*) made from chickpeas is used to make *gatte,* dumplings flavored with asafoetida and other spices, and immered in a yogurt-based gravy. This specialty of the city of Jaipur often is served with spinach (*gatte ka saag*). Spicy powdered lentils are used to make very thin, round wafers (*pappadam*) that are flame-roasted or deep-fried and eaten like chips as a snack or with a meal. Pickled fruits and vegetables are important substitutes for fresh foods out of season.

Much of the regional cuisine of Rajasthan reflects the former lifestyle of the community of Rajputs, members of warrior clans. The meal called *dal batti churma* kept well for days when the warriors went to battle in the desert. It consists of three separate dishes. The *dal,* a mixture of one or more lentils slow-cooked in clarified butter, is eaten with *batti,* a small, dense whole-wheat roll that is pressed to crack open its crust and drizzled with clarified butter. The third meal component, *churma,* is a caramelized, crumbly mixture of pulverized *batti* baked with powdered sugar or raw sugar and melted clarified butter. The meat-eating Rajputs were game hunters and their grilled meat specialties such as meat on skewers (*sula ka maas*) re still enjoyed today—but prepared with lamb or chicken because India bans hunting.

Madhya Pradish is the geographical heartland of India. The chain of hills running through it from east to west, the Vindhyas, divides the country into

Chakli, a deep-fried, delightfully light and crunchy snack made of rice flour and chickpea flour dough, which is extruded from a press. This popular spiral-shaped treat is typically made in homes for festivals. Drawn from *The Cooking of India,* by Santha Rama Rau.

northern and southern regions. Much of the state lies on a high plateau and is inhabited primarily by Hindus, with minority communities of Muslims, Jains, Sikhs and Christians. Major crops of the state are millet, legumes, peanuts, rice, sugar cane, wheat and sorghum. Popular foods include *bafla,* steamed wheat cakes immersed in clarified butter, similar to the baked *batti* of Rajasthan, and an assortment of *namkeen,* savory, salty snacks.

Western India

Western India encompasses the coastal states of Gujarat, Maharashtra and Goa. The northwestern part of the state of Gujarat, called the Kutch, is an isolated desert region with a large salt marsh. Gujarat's Kathiawar peninsula is marked by flat, barren plains and its fertile mainland is flanked on the south by the Western Ghats, the mountain range that runs along the western coast of India. Main crops are rice, wheat, millet, tobacco and cotton. Not surprisingly, the textile mills of Gujarat are famous all over India.

Almost all Gujaratis are strict vegetarians. Most residents are Hindus, but the state is also a major center for the Jains, an influential and wealthy community. Practitioners of non-violence, they avoid injury to life by adhering to rigid dietary restrictions. Gujaratis like their food sweet and spicy. Many of their recipes for savory dishes include some sugar, especially raw sugar.

Some regional dishes are *aloo shak,* a dish of potatoes stir-fried in spices and oil, Gujarati *kadhi,* a sweetened yogurt and chickpea-flour curry, and *osaman,* lentils cooked in tamarind water. Popular snacks include *dhokla,* steamed cakes made from a batter of lightly fermented rice flour and ground lentils, mixed with a spice paste, and *khandvi,* rolled strips of chickpea flour "pancakes" topped with chopped cilantro, grated coconut and a sautéed mixture of curry leaves, asafoetida and chopped green chile peppers. A variety of crunchy, fried snacks called *farsan* are largely based on beans and lentils, and are a part of snack mixtures called *chewda.*

Some Gujarati breads are *besan thepla,* a soft, flat, griddle-cooked bread made from chickpea flour, wheat flour and millet flour mixed with spices, herbs and yogurt; *batloo,* a flat, griddle-fried bread made with millet flour; and *khakhra roti,* a crispy, thin bread made from whole-wheat and white flours flavored with *garam masala* and roasted on a hot griddle. A pale green version of *khakhra roti* is made with finely chopped fenugreek leaves.

Well-known sweets to sample are *doodh pak,* a creamy rice dessert with ground cardamom, and *churma laddo,* a ball-shaped morsel made with whole-wheat flour, grated coconut and poppy seed.

Maharashtra is a large agricultural state. Much of it lies on the Deccan Plateau. Rice paddies and coconut palms dominate the landscape along its fertile Konkan coast. Major inland crops include rice, wheat, sorghum, millet, legumes, peanuts, sugar cane and cotton. The state is commercially developed and has a large industrial port city, Mumbai (Bombay), as its capital. The population is primarily Hindu. Among its minority communities are the Parsis (Persians), descendents of a community of people known as Zoroastrians, who practiced the beliefs of the prophet Zarathustra in eastern Persia. They emigrated to India to escape persecution by Muslim Arabs in Iran beginning in the eighth century.

Like the Gujaratis, Maharastrians prefer sweet and spicy food. They enjoy the fruit of the sea, especially *bombil,* the marine lizardfish known as Bombay duck, and pomfret. *Sarangya che bhujane* is a local specialty dish of pomfret slices cooked in a mixture of onions, ginger-garlic paste, cilantro and spices. *Gaboli* is dish of fish roe in a thick curry sauce. The Kolhapur Maharastrians, once warriors and game hunters, are meat eaters. One of their specialties is *mutton kolhapuri,* a dish of spicy lamb. The Parsis, also meat eaters, have added many unique dishes to the Indian kitchen. One of the most well known is *dhansak,* a one-dish meal containing chunks of lamb, vegetables

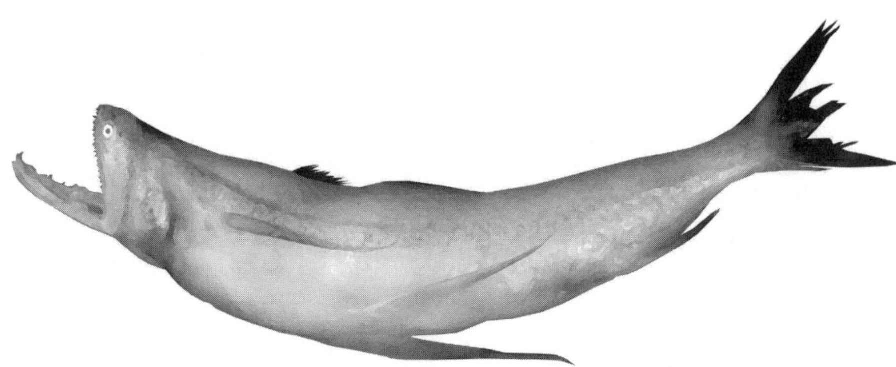

Bombay duck (*bombil*), a regional fish caught in the waters off the coast of Mumbai (Bombay). It is eaten fresh or dried for consumption during the monsoon season when fishing is impossible.

and several kinds of lentils, served with caramelized rice. Maharashtrian vegetarian dishes include *pavta batata,* a preparation of potatoes with lima beans. Dishes from the Konkan coast are laced with fresh coconut. Popular snacks relished, especially in Mumbai, are *vada pan,* a ball of spicy potato mixture covered with seasoned chickpea batter and fried, and *bhel puri,* a mixture of puffed rice, thin wafers made of lentils, deep-fried vermicelli, potatoes, onions, raw mango and various chutneys. Perhaps the most savored desserts are *puran poli,* a griddle-cooked sweet made of small circles of dough filled with a paste of lentils and raw sugar, and *shrikhand,* a sweet mixture of saffron- and cardamom-favored yogurt, garnished with pistachios or *chirongi,* lentil-sized brown fruit kernels from a tree of the cashew family.

The city of Mumbai has an ingenious and nearly infallible lunchtime meal distribution system to accommodate over 200,000 office workers who prefer meals that come from home. Each day some 5,000 carriers pick up carefully coded lunch boxes (*tiffins*) from suburban residences. Using various means of transportation, from bicycles to commuter trains, and always moving at a frenetic pace, they manage to punctually deliver each *tiffin* to the right office in the heart of the city. It is an amazing feat. After lunch, the boxes are returned by the same route.

The tiny and serene state of Goa is nestled between the Arabian Sea and the Western Ghats mountain range. Its primary religions are Hinduism and Christianity (mostly Roman Catholic), with Hinduism in the majority. Some of the more important crops grown in Goa are sugar cane, coconut, cashew, millet and rice. The state's unique culinary legacy stems from over four centuries of Portuguese domination.

The staple foods in both Hindu and Catholic households are rice, fish and spicy coconut curries. The rivers and sea provide a plentiful catch of shrimp, sardines, crabs, clams, mussels, lobsters, mackerel, kingfish and pomfret.

Hindu and Christian cookery are very different. Hindu cooking was not strongly influenced by Portuguese. Hindus avoid eating pork and beef, both of which are much appreciated by the Catholics. Hindus cook with raw sugar made from sugar cane, asafoetida, mustard seeds and fenugreek seeds. They use a type of lentil (*urad dal*) to ferment their batters, tamarind water to provide tartness, and several types of red chile pepper. Dried red mango rind is used to make the cold coconut-milk drink called *sol kadhi*. The Catholic larder has raw sugar made from palm sap, palm vinegar to ferment batters or to provide tartness, and a specific variety of plump, dried red chile peppers. One dish made in both Hindu and Catholic communities is *xacuti*. The meat, usually chicken or lamb, is marinated in a green spice paste containing green chile peppers, ginger, garlic and cilantro, and cooked in onions, tomatoes, a roasted spice mixture and freshly ground coconut. In Catholic households the dish will be much less spicy.

In the previous chapter we mentioned some Indian dishes influenced by Portuguese colonization. Some other famous Goan dishes with a Portuguese flavor are *sorpotel, a* spicy and vinegary dish of pork and liver, *para,* a pickled dried fish, and *pastelão,* a pork pie. Dessert perfections include *alebele,* pancakes filled with a spiced coconut mixture, and *bebinca,* a rich cake traditionally made of 16 layers, baked one layer at a time.

Southern India

The states of Andhra Pradesh, Karnataka, Tamil Nadu and Kerala comprise southern India. Because this area of India was not conquered by invading Muslims, the food shows little Moghlai influence, except in Andhra Pradesh.

You probably will have a chance to enjoy a special-occasion meal traditionally served on a banana leaf (the botanical *thali*), and you will see that the components of the repast have a specific position on the leaf in relation to each other, with regional variations, of course. Only the end of a banana leaf is used, and the narrow tip of the leaf typically will be on the left.

Andhra Pradesh is situated largely on the semi-arid Deccan Plateau. To the east is the lush coastal plain, and in the northeast, forming the eastern edge of the Deccan Plateau, are the mountains of the Eastern Ghats. Principal crops are rice, peanuts, millet, legumes, sugar cane and cotton. Most of the inhabitants are Hindus, with Muslims comprising the next largest religious group.

Andhra food is the hottest in India. Dishes are liberally laced with locally grown red and green chile peppers and an ample dollop of spices. Cinnamon, cloves and cardamom often are used whole. The usual antidote for counteracting the spiciness of food is cooling yogurt. The cuisine is predominantly vegetarian, except in the coastal areas where seafood is prevalent and in certain regions where meat became important. A typical meal includes rice served with *sambar,* a dish of lentils with vegetables, along with the notoriously hot Andhra chutneys and pickles such as *avakai thoku,* a fiery-hot mango pickle. Curried green chile peppers, *mirchi ka salan,* is a fiery vegetarian offering.

Although Andhra is a southern state, some of its dishes exemplify rich and aromatic northern Indian non-vegetarian cuisine. This is especially evident in the twin capital cities of Hyderabad and Secunderabad, which were home to Muslim rulers (Nawabs). The Moghul rulers from the north penetrated as far south as Hyderabad and left behind a culinary legacy. *Biryani,* perhaps the most spectacular and exotic of Moghlai dishes, is an elaborate layered dish of meat and saffron-flavored rice usually partaken with a spicy eggplant dish, *baghare baigan*. *Haleem,* a spicy porridge-like mixture of minced meat and cracked wheat topped with caramelized onions, is a specialty enjoyed during Ramadan at the end of the daily fast. Such a dish is likely to be made with lamb, the most-often used meat in non-vegetarian preparations. *Lukmi* is a dish of deep-fried squares of dough made of all-purpose flour and clarified butter, filled with a savory minced lamb mixture.

Ashrafi is a fancy sweet in Andhra. This coin-shaped morsel made of almond paste and thickened milk is flavored with saffron. A small ball of dough is pressed between two gold coins and bears their inscription. Don't miss the tasty *badam ki jaali,* a sandwich cookie with serrated edges, filled with sweetened almond paste. Another distinctive sweet is *khubani ka meetha,* a dish of stewed, dried apricots sprinkled with almonds and topped with cream.

Traditional Indian *tiffin* (lunchbox) with several round, stainless steel containers stacked on top of each other. Lunch typically includes rice, a lentil dish, vegetables, bread, pickles and a sweet. Each item has its own container, and its position in the stack varies between regions of the country. Drawn from *Great Curries of India,* by Camellia Panjabi.

Karnataka is situated on the western edge of the Deccan Plateau. The strip of land bordering on the Arabian Sea, known as the Malabar Coast, is backed by the Western Ghats mountain ranges. Coffee is the major crop. Tea, cotton, millet, cardamom, black pepper, cashews, sorghum and areca nut (betel nut) grow here as well. Although Hinduism is the major religion, significant numbers of Christians, Muslims and Jains live in Karnataka.

The culinary fare of Karnataka is typically vegetarian. Staple grains are rice, red millet and sorghum; coconut milk and oil are essential culinary ingredients. One of the state's most celebrated dishes is *bisibella bath,* a rice and lentil dish with mixed vegetables, red chile peppers, mustard seeds and lemon juice. Along the seacoast, fish and seafood are staples, and meat is on the menu as well. *Kane,* or ladyfish, is a delicacy especially favored in the coastal city of Mangalore in the southern part of the state. A local wild spinach called *besale* is also savored there. Popular breakfast offerings are *uppittu,* spicy roasted semolina, and *kuttige,* a rice and lentil (*urad dal*) batter steamed in jackfruit leaves. Favorite sweets include *godi halva* (*halwa*), made with bananas and wheat flour; *malpua,* a round, sugar-soaked treat with a spongy center, made from a batter of flour, semolina and milk; and *mysore pak,* a fudge-like delicacy from the city of Mysore that is made from chickpea flour mixed with clarified butter and cooked in boiling sugar syrup.

Tamil Nadu is located at the southern tip of India. Its eastern boundary lies on the Coromandel coast. A short stretch of the western boundary of the state lies on the Malabar coast. The mountain ranges comprising the Eastern and Western Ghats meet in Tamil Nadu and run along its eastern and western borders. The state is largely agricultural, producing rice, coffee, tea, sesame, mustard, legumes, millet, coconut, tamarind, peanuts and cotton, which is used to make the famous madras cloth. Most of the people practice Hinduism. The Brahmins are vegetarians, but other Hindus eat the readily available fish and seafood, and meat other than beef. Christianity and Islam also are major religions in the state.

The main staple is rice, which often is parboiled. The fertile plains of central Tamil Nadu grow *ponni,* a long-grain rice used in a variety of dishes, and a black rice used for puddings. Legumes and vegetables also are important standbys. Coconut, asafoetida and tamarind flavor many dishes. Hardly a meal lacks some *pappad* (*pappadam*), thin, round crisps made of ground lentils and spices. One of the specialties of Tamil Nadu is *milakai podi,* ground lentils, spices and oil, eaten with pieces of *idli,* a "cake" made from steamed, fermented rice and lentils (*urad dal*). Each component of this dish is served in a separate bowl and mixed together on a plate with the fingers. *Podi uthapam* (*uddapam*), is a type of *dosa* (crêpe made with soaked rice and lentils ground to a paste and fermented briefly for taste) with minced vegetables in the batter. It is a specialty of the states of Tamil Nadu and Karnatka. Some sweet treats of Tamil Nadu are *suiyam,* sweet, deep-fried balls made of lentils (*chana dal*), coconut and palm sugar; and a specialty of the city of Chennai called *kandarpam,* deep-fried balls of flour and raw sugar. *Pongal* is a pudding made of freshly harvested rice, milk and raw sugar, and also the name of the harvest festival. *Tayyar shaadum* is a mixture of rice and yogurt enjoyed at the end of a meal to settle the stomach. Coffee brewed from beans grown on local hillside plantations is the most popular beverage.

In southeastern Tamil Nadu the Chettinad region is home to a Hindu community of prosperous bankers and traders, whose members are known as the Nattukottai Chettiars. Chettinad cuisine is hot, spicy and non-vegetarian. One of their better known specialties is *chettinad ka mirch murga,*a peppery chicken dish.

Kerala is a long, narrow state along the southwestern coast of the Indian peninsula, bordered by the Arabian Sea along the Malabar Coast, and rimmed on the east by the Western Ghats mountains. The state has a great many lakes and rivers connected by man-made canals to transport agricultural products to the ports. Important crops are cardamom, chile peppers, cashews, coconut, turmeric, black pepper, rice, nutmeg, mace, tea, tapioca, cinnamon and ginger. Most Keralites are Hindus, but some are Muslims, Christians and Jews.

The cuisine of Kerala includes richly spiced vegetarian and non-vegetarian dishes with regional and religious variations. Only orthodox Brahmin Hindus eschew meat. Most dishes are flavored with curry leaves, coconut and tamarind. Rice, the staple food, is boiled and served plain with spicy sauces, commonly thickened with coconut milk. Batters made from this treasured grain are transformed into a variety of crêpes, "cakes" and noodles. *Dosa* is a crispy crêpe made with soaked rice and and a type of lentil (*urad dal*) ground to a paste and fermented briefly for taste. This specialty usually is filled with a dry vegetable mixture. Typically accompanying it are coconut chutney and *sambar,* a southern Indian dish of lentils with vegetables. *Idiappam* are steamed noodles made by extruding a batter of ground rice through a special press. This popular breakfast item, also called "string hoppers," is enjoyed with sweetened coconut milk. *Appam* is a crêpe made of rice and coconut milk cooked in a special round-bottomed pan, giving the crêpe thin, lacy sides and a thicker bottom. Traditionally it is served hot with gravy dishes. This version of a crêpe is attributed to the Syrian Christians, who have been in southern India since the 300s, having emigrated from Baghdad and Jerusalem to escape religious persecution. *Alisa* is a crêpe made from ground rice and *urad dal*, topped with a shredded meat mixture, and rolled. Two sides of the crêpe are folded to the center before rolling to help keep the contents from spilling out. The roll is then fried in a little vegetable oil. It is a traditional starter dish in the Mopillah Muslim community of northern Kerala.

Keralite vegetarians enjoy *avial*, a dish of cooked vegetables cut in uniform 1-inch pieces, served in a yogurt and coconut sauce. Potatoes, yams, carrots, gourds, plaintain, jackfruit, green beans and drumsticks, the green pods of the Indian horseradish tree, typically are used in *avial*. Fish and seafood are bountiful and relished. *Meen moiley,* fish in a creamy coconut sauce, is a classic dish, as is *chemeen pappas,* shrimp in coconut milk. *Chemeen varattiyathu,* shrimp in tamarind sauce, and *thenga chor,* rice cooked in coconut milk with mussels, are special recipes of the Mopillah Muslim community. *Chuttulli meen,* fish marinated in onions and spices, is a traditional dish from the once-thriving Jewish community of Fort Cochin. *Beet khuta* is a sweet-and-sour curried chicken with beets. The recipe is associated with the Cochini Jewish community. *Payasam* is at the top of the sweets list. It is a milk-based dessert with rice or vermicelli, sugar and cashews. A darker version is made with palm sugar.

Eastern India

The states of Bihar, Orissa, Chhattisgarh, Jharkhand, West Bengal, Assam, Meghalaya, Arunachal Pradesh, Manipur, Nagaland, Mizoram, Tripura and Sikkim make up the eastern region of India. Chhattisgarh and Jharkhand are relatively new states. In 2000 Chhattisgarh was carved out of Madya Pradesh, Jharkhand out of Bihar.

Bihar is a rich agricultural area, crossed by the Ganges River. Among the crops grown are rice, sugar cane, wheat, corn, millet, barley, sesame, legumes, potatoes, tobacco and jute. The population is primarily Hindu, with minority communities of Muslims, Jains and several tribal groups.

The Biharis are vegetarians, but they do eat fish. A typical meal includes rice, legumes and *roti* (*chappati*), tortilla-like unleavened bread made with wheat flour and baked on an ungreased griddle. Several different kinds of *kachori,* deep-fried breads with a savory filling, are popular. An important staple is a powder called *sattu,* which is ground from black chickpeas (*kala chana*), certain lentils, rice or barley. It is combined with water, sugar, lemon juice and black salt to make a cooling summer beverage. Roasted *sattu,* green chile peppers, garlic, onion, ginger and *ajwain* seeds form a stuffing for a griddle-baked wheat bun to make *litti.* This tasty stuffed bun is rolled in clarified butter and eaten with *baingan bharta,* a dish of roasted, puréed eggplant. A favorite breakfast dish is *chura dahi,* cooked and flattened rice mixed with raw sugar and yogurt.

The state of Jharkhand, which comprises the former southern portion of the state of Bihar, has an agricultural economy. It is a large fruit-growing area, producing crops of citrus fruits, litchi, mango, banana and guava. Other crops include legumes, rice, corn and wheat. The population primarily consists of tribal communities.

The maritime state of Orissa lies on the Bay of Bengal. About three fourths of the state is covered by rugged hills and forest. The fertile coastal plains annually produce two crops of rice. Red millet, wheat, and corn are grown in the rolling uplands. Other important crops are legumes, sugar cane, coconut, turmeric, mustard seeds, peanuts, cashews and sesame. The overwhelming majority of people are Hindu, with small minorities of Muslims and Christians.

Orissan cuisine is characterized by the generous use of yogurt, coconut and mustard seeds. *Dalma,* a spicy dish of chopped vegetables, fruits and coconut cooked with split yellow lentils (*arhar dal*), is a popular dish served with steamed rice. Sweet and savory cakes called *pithas* are a typical festival food. They are made with lentils (*urad dal*) or semolina, raw sugar and coconut, with any number of additional components. *Besare* is a dish of vegetables cooked with a mustard seed mixture. The diet is rich in fish, especially pomfret, and seafood—crab, lobster and shrimp. Meat consumption is relatively low. A regional dessert specialty made with farmer's cheese and sugar syrup is called is *chhenapodapitha.*

The state of Chhattisgarh was created from the former southeastern portion of the state of Madhya Pradesh in 2000. Agriculture is the mainstay of the economy. Primary crops are rice, corn, legumes, sorghum, potatoes, eggplant and tomatoes. Rice is the dietary staple, supplemented with fish and pork. Tribal communities make up most of the population.

West Bengal stretches from the Himalayas in the north to the Bay of Bengal in the south. Most Bengalis are Hindus, with minority populations of

Muslims and tribal peoples. Principal crops are legumes, rice, sugar cane, wheat, tea and fruits such as mangoes, coconuts and bananas. Large fields of black mustard are testimony to the Bengali love of mustard as a spice and source of cooking oil. Mustard seeds are one of five ingredients in the colorful, aromatic spice blend called *panch phoron,* which gives Bengali cuisine its characteristic aroma. The other ingredients of *panch phoron* are fennel seeds, fenugreek seeds, cumin seeds and black nigella seeds (*klonji*), also identified as black caraway and black onion seeds. These spices are mixed in equal proportions and used whole or ground. Lentils are the basis of a traditional local food called *bori.* Water-soaked lentils are ground to a paste and mixed with spices. Bite-size pieces of the dough are dried in the sun, then fried in oil. Bori added to stews or crumbled over vegetables adds texture and flavor.

Fish, rice and world-class milk-based sweets are Bengali specialities. A regional fish dish, is *bhalolaga illisher paturi,* is made with *illisher* (*hilsa*), a popular fish found in the estuaries of the Bay of Bengal. The fish is marinated in mustard oil and spices, wrapped in banana leaves and steamed. The mustardy, oily sauce produced in the cooking process is served with rice. *Bekti jhol* is a favorite way to cook another beloved Bengali fish, the boneless *bekti,* which is stewed with potatoes, pointed gourd and green bananas in a spicy, thin gravy flavored with cilantro. A vegetarian specialty is Bengali *khatta mitha chana dal,* a sweet-and-sour lentil dish made with a type of lentil called *chana dal.* It is a thick mixture of cooked lentils sweetened with sugar and drizzled with *panch phoron*. *Paratha,* a flat, unleavened, triangular-shaped bread made of wheat flour and clarified butter, is called *parota* in West Bengal. A more elaborate local version of this bread, *dhakai parota,* is round and multilayerd, and is enjoyed with curries. *Luchi* is a deep-fried bread made from wheat flour and clarified butter. Circles are cut out of thinly rolled dough and fried in oil. The bread puffs up like a balloon as hot oil is spooned over the top of it. In other parts of the country this bread is called *puri.* Bengalis have a dessert they are especially passionate about: *mishti doi,* made by adding yogurt and sugar to fresh milk that has been partially condensed by boiling. The mixture sets when cooled. It traditionally is prepared in clay bowls.

The Himalayan state of Sikkim was annexed in 1975. Its economy is essentially agrarian. Major crops include rice, wheat, millet, corn, barley and fruit. Over half of the population is Hindu. Sikkim's cuisine is an amalgam of Tibetan, Bhutanese, Nepali and Chinese food.

The area of the seven northeastern states of Assam, Meghalaya, Arunachal Pradesh, Manipur, Nagaland, Mizoram and Tripura stretches from Tibet in the north to Myanmar in the south. These are tribal states making up what is often referred to as the "seven sisters." The states are not often visited by foreigners, and many of their tribal communities are scarcely known to the western world. Assam, the most widely known of the seven states, produces the much-savored assam and darjeeling varieties of tea. Much remains to be discovered about this remote region of India.

Tastes of India

You are encouraged to prepare some of these delicious, traditional Indian recipes before leaving home. This is a wonderful and immediately satisfying way to preview the extraordinary cuisine of India. Most of the special ingredients needed to make these dishes can be obtained in the United States (see *Resources,* p. 71). Satisfactory substitutes are given for those that are unavailable. Not surprisingly, some dishes have an English name or one that includes English word(s), testimony to British rule of the country for over 300 years.

Appetizers

Galawat Kabab

Melt-in-the-mouth kebab. Serves 4–5.

This recipe was contributed by Gulam Rasool, executive chef at the Taj Residency Hotel in Lucknow, Uttar Pradesh. The meat is tenderized with papaya, which historically was used to make it more chewable for certain toothless Nawabs (rulers) of Lucknow. Traditionally a main dish, it is now a starter course.

1 SMALL PAPAYA

1⅓ POUNDS LAMB, FINELY MINCED

3 TABLESPOONS VEGETABLE OIL

1½-INCH PIECE FRESH GINGER

2 MEDIUM CLOVES GARLIC

¼ CUP CHICKPEA FLOUR, DRY-ROASTED UNTIL GOLDEN

½ TEASPOON CAYENNE PEPPER, OR TO TASTE

SALT TO TASTE

Galawat masala (*spice mixture*)

3 PODS BLACK CARDAMOM, USE SEEDS ONLY

½ TEASPOON BLACK PEPPERCORNS

[Galawat Kebab, *continued*]

¼ TEASPOON GROUND CLOVES

½ TEASPOON MACE

¼ TEASPOON CARDAMOM POWDER

½ TEASPOON CINNAMON POWDER

½ TEASPOON NUTMEG POWDER

1 HOT COAL FOR SMOKING MEAT (PREPARE OUTDOORS)

¼ TEASPOON CLARIFIED BUTTER (*GHEE*)*

1 ONION, FINELY SLICED

1 LEMON, CUT IN WEDGES

2 THIN, HOT GREEN CHILE PEPPERS, CUT IN JULIENNE

Grind papaya into a paste. In a sturdy metal bowl, mix meat with 2 tablespoons of papaya paste and 2 tablespoons of vegetable oil. Let stand for 30 minutes. Grind garlic and ginger together into a paste, and add to meat, along with chickpea flour, cayenne pepper and salt. Finely grind the *galawat masala* ingredients together and add to the meat, mixing well. Make a mound of the meat and form a depression in the middle. Take outdoors and place a hot coal on a piece of foil in the depression and put clarified butter on top of the coal. Cover bowl immediately with foil and keep covered for 15 minutes. This will impart a unique smoky flavor to the meat. Uncover bowl; carefully remove coal and extinguish it. Finish preparation indoors. Make round patties about 3 inches in diameter. Heat 1 tablespoon of vegetable oil in a shallow pan over high heat and fry patties for 1 minute. Reduce heat to medium and continue frying patties on both sides until well done. Serve with onion, lemon and green chiles.

*Available at Indian and specialty food markets; also see *Resources,* p. 71, for mail-order suppliers of Indian food.

Side Dishes

Nimbu Chaval

Lemon rice. Serves 2–3.

The recipe for this southern Indian dish was provided by Veena Arora, chef at the Spice Route Restaurant in the Imperial Hotel in New Delhi.

1 TABLESPOON VEGETABLE OIL

½ TEASPOON MUSTARD SEEDS

½ TEASPOON *URAD DAL* (TYPE OF LENTIL)*

½ TEASPOON *CHANA DAL* (TYPE OF LENTIL)*

20 CURRY LEAVES*

2–3 WHOLE, SMALL, DRIED, HOT RED CHILE PEPPERS

3 THIN, HOT GREEN CHILE PEPPERS, DESEEDED (OPTIONAL) AND COARSELY CHOPPED

1 TABLESPOON CASHEW NUT PIECES

½ TEASPOON GRATED FRESH GINGER

½ TEASPOON TURMERIC

1 TABLESPOON LEMON JUICE

SALT TO TASTE

2 CUPS COOKED WHITE RICE (A NON-AROMATIC VARIETY)

Heat oil in frying pan over high heat until shimmering. Add mustard seeds, cover pan and let sputter. When sputtering slows down, lower heat to medium. Add lentils, curry leaves, red and green chiles, cashew nuts and ginger, and fry until the lentils become slightly golden brown. Remove pan from heat. Take out half the curry leaves and set aside for the garnish. Blend in turmeric, lemon juice and salt. Add rice and mix well. Transfer to a serving bowl and garnish with curry leaves.

*Available at Indian and specialty food markets; also see *Resources,* p. 71, for mail-order suppliers of Indian food.

Ananas Sassam

Pineapple curry. Serves 2.

This recipe was contributed by Ananda Solomon, chef at the Konkan Café in the President Hotel in Mumbai. The dish is traditionally sweetened with *jaggery,* a dark brown or yellow unrefined sugar made from palm or sugarcane juice.

2 WHOLE, SMALL, DRIED HOT RED CHILE PEPPERS

3 TABLESPOONS GRATED FRESH COCONUT

1 TABLESPOON VEGETABLE OIL

1 TEASPOON BLACK MUSTARD SEEDS

2 TABLESPOONS CHOPPED ONIONS

5–6 CURRY LEAVES*

¼ CUP DESEEDED AND CHOPPED TOMATOES

½ POUND FRESH PINEAPPLE, CUT INTO ABOUT ¾-INCH CUBES†

3 TABLESPOONS WATER

1 TEASPOON BROWN SUGAR

Grind chiles to a coarse powder, mix with coconut and set aside. Heat oil in a frying pan over high heat until shimmering. Add mustard seeds, cover pan and let

[Ananas Sassam, *continued*]
sputter. When sputtering slows down, lower heat to medium. Stir in onion, curry leaves, tomato and pineapple. Add 1 tablespoon water and cook for 3–5 minutes over medium heat. Add chile-coconut mixture, brown sugar and 2 tablespoons of water. Cover and cook over low heat for 5 minutes.
*Available at Indian and specialty food markets; also see *Resources,* p. 71, for mail-order suppliers of Indian food.

†Can substitute canned pineapple chunks of similar size, well drained.

Nariyal Palak

Spinach with coconut. Serves 2.

The recipe for this vegetable side dish was contributed by executive chef Cruz Urbano do Rego of the Taj Holiday Village, Goa.

- 1 TABLESPOON VEGETABLE OIL
- 1 TEASPOON MUSTARD SEEDS
- ¼ CUP FINELY CHOPPED ONION
- 1 POUND FRESH SPINACH (ABOUT 1 CUP COOKED)
- ¼ TEASPOON SALT
- ¼ CUP GRATED FRESH COCONUT

Wash spinach, drain and coarsely chop. Set aside. Heat oil in frying pan over high heat until shimmering. Add mustard seeds, cover pan and let sputter. When sputtering slows down, reduce heat to medium and add onion. Cook until translucent. Add spinach and salt, mixing well. Cook until done. Serve garnished with coconut.

Achariya Aloo

"Pickled" potatoes. Serves 2–3.

This recipe was provided by Vikramaditya Singh Sodawas, whose family owns the Karni group of hotels and restaurants featuring traditional Sodawas (western Ragasthan) family recipes.

- 4 TABLESPOONS VEGETABLE OIL
- ¼ TEASPOON ASAFOETIDA (*HING*)*
- 1½ CUPS POTATOES, CHOPPED INTO ½-INCH CUBES
- SALT TO TASTE
- ¼ TEASPOON TURMERIC
- 2 TABLESPOONS FRESH GINGER, CUT IN JULIENNE
- 2 TABLESPOONS FENUGREEK SEEDS, SOAKED IN WATER FOR 1 HOUR

1 TEASPOON NIGELLA SEEDS

1 TABLESPOON PAPRIKA

Heat oil in a wok or frying pan over high heat. Stir in asafoetida. Add potatoes, reduce heat to medium and shallow fry for a few minutes until almost cooked. Add salt. Fry for 10 more minutes, or until potatoes are cooked. Add turmeric, ginger, drained fenugreek seeds, nigella seeds and paprika, stirring after the addition of each ingredient. Stir for another 30 seconds. Serve hot.

*Available at Indian and specialty food markets; also see *Resources,* p. 71, for mail-order suppliers of Indian foods.

Enai Katrikey

Aromatic sautéed eggplant. Serves 4.

This recipe was contributed by chef P.K. Vikram Kumar of the Taj Garden Retreat Hotel, Madurai, in the state of Tamil Nadu.

4 TABLESPOONS VEGETABLE OIL

1½ POUNDS BABY EGGPLANTS, EACH CUT INTO 4 PIECES

1 SMALL ONION, CHOPPED

1 CLOVE GARLIC, SLICED

1 TABLESPOON GRATED FRESH GINGER

½ TEASPOON CUMIN SEEDS

1 TEASPOON BLACK MUSTARD SEEDS

½ TEASPOON BLACK PEPPERCORNS

1-INCH PIECE CINNAMON STICK

½ CUP GRATED FRESH COCONUT

4 DRIED, HOT RED CHILE PEPPERS

1 TABLESPOON CORIANDER SEEDS

2 TEASPOONS FENNEL SEEDS

1 TEASPOON STAR ANISE

4 WHOLE CASHEW NUTS

1 TABLESPOON COCONUT OIL

10 CURRY LEAVES

¼ TEASPOON TURMERIC

½ TEASPOON SALT

¾ CUP WATER

[Enai Katrikey, *continued*]

Heat oil in frying pan and sauté eggplant until soft. Remove from pan and set aside. Fry onion, garlic and ginger for 1–2 minutes over high heat, and set aside. In same pan, dry roast cumin, ½ teaspoon mustard seeds, peppercorns, cinnamon, coconut, two red chile peppers, coriander, fennel, star anise and cashew nuts until dark brown. Let cool. Grind dry-roasted spices with fried onion, garlic, ginger, and ¼ cup water into a fine paste and set aside.

Heat coconut oil in frying pan over high heat until shimmering. Add ½ teaspoon mustard seeds, two red chile peppers and curry leaves. Cover pan and let seeds sputter. When sputtering slows down, remove spices from pan and set aside. Return partly cooked eggplant to pan. Add turmeric, salt, spice paste and ½ cup water. Mix well and cook 5 minutes over medium heat or until eggplant is completely cooked. Garnish with fried mustard seeds, red chile peppers and curry leaves.

Palak Paneer

Spinach with farmer's cheese. Serves 4.

The recipe for this dish was contributed by Preeti Vaid, a radiologist and resident of Delhi. It is a northern Indian dish that is popular throughout India.

2 MEDIUM CLOVES GARLIC

1½-INCH PIECE FRESH GINGER

1 POUND FRESH SPINACH, WASHED

½ CUP WATER

2 TABLESPOONS VEGETABLE OIL

½ TEASPOON CUMIN SEEDS

1 CUP PURÉED ONION (ABOUT 1 LARGE ONION)

½ POUND FARMER'S CHEESE, CUT INTO ¾-INCH CUBES*

¼ TEASPOON TURMERIC

¼ TEASPOON CAYENNE PEPPER, OR TO TASTE

1 TEASPOON GROUND CORIANDER

SALT TO TASTE

1 CUP FINELY CHOPPED TOMATOES

Cut garlic and ginger into small pieces, grind together into a paste and set aside. Add spinach to boiling water and cover. Reduce heat and simmer for 5 minutes, stirring occasionally. Cool and purée. In a frying pan, heat oil over medium heat. Add cumin and fry for about 30 seconds. Add onion and cook about 5 minutes until the mixture begins to clump together. Add the garlic-ginger paste and fry until the mixture is golden brown, about 5 minutes. Stir in turmeric, cayenne pepper, coriander and salt, and fry a few more minutes. Add tomatoes and cook over high heat until the tomatoes are well puréed. Add spinach and cheese and cook, covered, over medium-low heat for about 10 minutes.

*See p. 67 for a recipe for the farmer's cheese used in this recipe.

Bean Poriyal

Green beans with coconut. Serves 6–8.

This recipe was provided by Joan Peterson, co-author of this guidebook. It was given to her by Narasima Katari when they both attended graduate school at the University of Wisconsin. It has remained a family favorite for years.

2 POUNDS FRESH GREEN BEANS, CUT FRENCH-STYLE*

2 TABLESPOONS OIL

½ TEASPOON BLACK MUSTARD SEEDS

1 TEASPOON LENTILS (*URAD DAL*)†

1 MEDIUM ONION, FINELY CHOPPED

2 THIN, HOT GREEN CHILE PEPPERS, FINELY CHOPPED

½ TEASPOON SALT, OR TO TASTE

¼ CUP GRATED FRESH COCONUT

1 TABLESPOON FRESH LEMON JUICE

SLICED ALMONDS

Cook beans in water without salt until tender, drain well and set aside. Heat oil in frying pan over high heat until shimmering. Add mustard seeds, cover pan and let sputter. When sputtering slows down, reduce heat to medium and add lentils. Fry uncovered until brown, being careful not to burn them. Mix in onion and chile peppers, and sauté until limp. Add beans and salt, stirring well. Turn off heat and add coconut, tossing well with other ingredients. Mix in lemon juice and sprinkle surface with almonds.

*Frozen French-style green beans can be substituted. Cook beans per package directions, omiting the salt. Drain well.

†Available at Indian and specialty food markets; also see *Resources,* p. 71, for mail-order suppliers of Indian foods.

Avial

Vegetables in coconut and yogurt sauce. Serves 8.

The recipe for this southern Indian dish was contributed by Shoba Mohan, from Visakhapatnam in the state of Andhra Pradesh, and her mother-in-law, Mrs. Rajam

[Avial, *continued*]

Nagarajan, from the state of Kerala. Shoba and her husband, Mohan (P.N. Narayanaswamy), are co-owners of Travel Scope, the travel agency based in New Delhi that handles the culinary tour to India led by the authors of this book.

Typical vegetables used in this dish include potatoes, yams, carrots, gourds, plantains, peas, drumsticks,* green beans and fava beans. Vegetables are cut into 1-inch pieces of even thickness.

2 TEASPOONS COCONUT OIL

1 CUP PEAS, FRESH OR FROZEN

1 CUP YAMS

1 CUP PEELED PLANTAIN

4 CUPS WATER

1 CUP CARROTS

1 CUP PUMPKIN

1 CUP GREEN BEANS

1 CUP WINTER SQUASH

1 SPRIG CURRY LEAVES (ABOUT 12 LEAVES)

½ TEASPOON SALT, OR TO TASTE

Yogurt sauce

2 CUPS YOGURT

1 CUP GRATED FRESH COCONUT

2 THIN, HOT GREEN CHILE PEPPERS (ABOUT 2–3 INCHES LONG)

1 TEASPOON CUMIN SEEDS

Heat oil over low heat in a deep, heavy pot. Add vegetables that take longer to cook first (peas, yams and plaintain) and water, and cook, covered, for 6–8 minutes over high heat. Mix in remaining vegetables, curry leaves and salt. Cook until the vegetables are just done. Remove from heat and cool slightly.

To make the sauce, put yogurt, coconut, chile peppers and cumin in a blender and mix to a smooth paste. Add sauce to cooked vegetables and mix gently until the sauce covers the vegetables. Serve with steamed rice and *appalams* (*pappadums*), 6-inch round wafers made from a type of lentil called *urad dal*.† In southern India, these wafers typically are deep-fried in oil.

*Drumsticks (*sahjan*) are the long, slender, green pods of the Indian horseradish tree (*Moringa oleifera*). The thin layer of "meat" surrounding the pod's round seeds is edible.

†Available at Indian and specialty food markets; also see *Resources,* p. 71, for mail-order suppliers of Indian foods.

Moong Ussul

Sprouted mung beans. Serves 2.

The recipe for this Goan side dish was provided by Alphonso Pereira, executive chef at the Rio-Rico Restaurant in the Hotel Mondavi in Panaji, Goa.

1 CUP DRIED MUNG BEANS, SPROUTED*

1 TABLESPOON PEANUT OIL

1 TEASPOON MUSTARD SEEDS

1 SPRIG CURRY LEAVES (ABOUT 12 LEAVES)

¼ TEASPOON ASAFOETIDA (*HING*) (OPTIONAL)†

1 TEASPOON CHOPPED, THIN, HOT GREEN CHILE PEPPERS, OR TO TASTE

PINCH OF SUGAR

SALT TO TASTE

¼ CUP GRATED FRESH COCONUT

Cover beans with water, bring to a boil and reduce heat to medium. Cook for 5 minutes. If desired, cook an additional 15 minutes to remove outer green skin. Drain and set aside. Heat oil in frying pan over high heat until shimmering. Add mustard seeds, cover pan and let sputter. When sputtering slows down, reduce heat to medium and stir in curry leaves, asafoetida, chile pepper and sugar. Add beans, salt and coconut. Cook until beans are no longer crunchy, about 5 minutes. Serve hot or at room temperature.

*Plan ahead. Allow 2–3 days for the beans to sprout. To sprout beans, soak overnight in water. Next day, place soaked, drained beans in a jar. Cover top of jar with cheesecloth and hold in place with a rubber band. Invert jar, place in bowl and put in a dark place. Twice a day fill jar with water, drain and invert jar as before. Continue until sprouts are 1 to 1½ inches long.

†Available at Indian and specialty food markets; also see *Resources,* p. 71, for mail-order suppliers of Indian foods.

Kheera Raita

Cucumber in yogurt. Serves 4–6.

The recipe for this popular side dish was provided by Indu Menon, co-author of this guidebook. It is enjoyed as a cooling accompaniment to peppery dishes.

1 CUP GRATED CUCUMBER

1½ CUPS PLAIN, WHOLE-MILK YOGURT

¼ TEASPOON SALT

[Kheera Raita, *continued*]

- 1/8 TEASPOON CAYENNE PEPPER
- 1/4 TEASPOON CUMIN SEEDS

Dry roast the cumin seeds in a small frying pan until they turn dark brown. Cool, then coarsely grate. Mix all ingredients together in a serving bowl. Serve chilled.

Main Dishes

Dal Makhani

Buttery dal. Serves 2.

The recipe for this gravy-like dish was contributed by chef J.P. Singh from the ITC Maurya Sheraton in Delhi. It is one of the signature preparations of the hotel's Bukhara Restaurant, which features the cuisine of the Northwest Frontier.

- 4 OUNCES WHOLE (BLACK-SKINNED) LENTILS (*URAD DAL*)
- 5¼ CUPS WATER FOR COOKING
- 7 TABLESPOONS UNSALTED BUTTER
- ½ CUP TOMATO PURÉE
- ¼ TEASPOON CAYENNE PEPPER, OR TO TASTE
- 1½-INCH PIECE FRESH GINGER
- 2 MEDIUM GARLIC CLOVES
- ¼ CUP WHIPPING CREAM*

Pick over lentils for stones and wash 4–5 times with water. Soak lentils overnight in enough water to cover them. Next day, drain and bring to a boil in 4 cups water. Reduce heat and simmer, covered, until lentils become soft but still retain black skin, about 1½ hours. Drain excess water and discard scum. Add butter, tomato, cayenne pepper and remaining 1¼ cups water, and mix well. Grind ginger and garlic together into a paste and stir into mixture. Simmer uncovered until lentils starts to get mushy and thick. Add cream and cook for another 15 minutes, covered. Serve hot with *naan* (leavened flatbread). See p. 63 for recipe to make *naan*.

*Half & half is not recommended because it tends to curdle.

Lal Maans (Maas)

Red lamb stew. Serves 6–8.

Rajeev Sharma, executive chef at the Samode Palace in the village of Samode, Rajasthan, contributed this recipe for the favorite Rajasthani lamb dish. Now a premier hotel, the palace had been the residence of the princes of the House of Kacchawaha Rajputs.

1 CUP WHOLE-MILK YOGURT

1 TABLESPOON COARSELY GROUND, SMALL, DRIED, HOT RED CHILE PEPPERS*

1 TABLESPOON PAPRIKA

1 TEASPOON DRY-ROASTED CUMIN SEEDS, GROUND

3 TABLESPOONS CORIANDER

1 TEASPOON TURMERIC

2 TEASPOONS SALT (OR TO TASTE)

4 TABLESPOONS VEGETABLE OIL

½ CUP SLIVERED GARLIC

2 CUPS FINELY SLICED ONIONS

5 PODS BLACK CARDAMOM, LIGHTLY CRUSHED

5 PODS GREEN CARDAMOM, LIGHTLY CRUSHED

3 POUNDS LEG OF LAMB, CUT INTO 1½- to 2-INCH CUBES

2–2½ CUPS WATER

1 CUP COARSELY CHOPPED CILANTRO

Whisk together yogurt, red pepper, paprika, cumin, coriander and 1½ teaspoon of salt, and set aside. Heat oil in heavy frying pan over medium heat. Add garlic and sauté until golden brown. Mix in the onion and black and green cardamom, and sauté until onion is golden brown. Add lamb and sauté 4–5 minutes. Add water and remaining salt.

Slowly blend in the yogurt mixture, stirring constantly. Bring to a boil, cover and simmer, stirring occasionally until the meat is tender, about 1½ hours. Adjust for salt. Transfer to a serving dish and garnish with chopped cilantro. Serve hot with *chappatis* (*phulkas*).

*The amount of red pepper called for in chef Sharma's recipe has been greatly reduced. Use even less, if desired. The authentic preparation, according to chef Sharma, is only for those with steel-lined stomachs.

Pittore

Chana dal *flour "dumplings" in yogurt sauce*. Serves 4.

The recipe for this Rajasthani specialty was provided by Man Singh Rathore and Durga Kanwar, their son, Harshvardhan Singh Rathore, and daughter-in-law, Shri

[Pittore, *continued*]

Nidhi. Their estate in Nimaj, Rajasthan, a hunting preserve known as Chhatra Sagar, has been in the family for generations.

"Dumplings"

1½ CUPS CHICKPEA FLOUR (*BESAN*)*

1 TEASPOON GROUND CUMIN

1 TEASPOON TURMERIC

½ TEASPOON CAYENNE PEPPER

½ TEASPOON SALT, OR TO TASTE

1 TEASPOON FINELY DICED, THIN, HOT GREEN CHILE PEPPERS

1 CUP WATER

2 TEASPOONS VEGETABLE OIL

Sauce

½ CUP WHOLE-MILK YOGURT

½ TEASPOON SALT

1 TEASPOON TURMERIC

4 TEASPOONS PAPRIKA

½ TEASPOON GRATED FRESH GINGER

¼ CUP VEGETABLE OIL

½ CUP THINLY SLICED ONION

1 TEASPOON MINCED GARLIC

3–4 GREEN CARDAMOM PODS, SLIGHTLY CRUSHED

Sift together flour, cumin, turmeric, cayenne pepper and salt. Add chile pepper and water, and mix until smooth. Heat vegetable oil in a frying pan over medium heat and add flour mixture. Cook for 10–15 minutes, stirring constantly. The mixture should become dough-like. Spread mixture evenly in a greased pie plate (9″ diameter), making a layer about ½-inch thick. Smooth surface with a spoon and let cool. Cut into 15–20 diamond-shaped pieces with a sharp knife.

Mix yogurt, salt, turmeric, paprika, and ginger in a bowl, and set aside. Heat oil in a saucepan over medium heat, and fry onion and garlic until golden. Add yogurt mixture, reduce heat and stir until mixture begins to simmer. Continue simmering for 10 minutes, or until the liquid thickens slightly. Add "dumplings" and cook for a few more minutes. Garnish with cardamom. Serve hot with *chappatis*.

*Can also use garbanzo bean flour (also called *besan;* garbanzo beans are larger than the Indian chickpea called *chana dal*). Available at Indian and specialty food markets; also see *Resources,* p. 71, for mail-order suppliers of Indian foods.

Kachhe Gosht ki Biryani

Classic lamb and rice dish. Serves 6–8.

Chef Chaman Lal Sharma of Taj Banjara, Hyderabad, provided the recipe for this traditional and elaborate Moghlai dish.

2 LARGE CLOVES GARLIC

1½-INCH PIECE FRESH GINGER

2 CUPS WHOLE-MILK YOGURT

1 TEASPOON *GARAM MASALA* (SPECIAL SPICE MIXTURE)*

¼ TEASPOON CAYENNE PEPPER

3 THIN, HOT GREEN CHILE PEPPERS, DESEEDED AND MINCED

¼ CUP COARSELY CHOPPED CILANTRO

¼ CUP COARSELY CHOPPED FRESH MINT

2 TEASPOONS SALT

1 TABLESPOON MINCED PAPAYA

1 TEASPOON TURMERIC

1 TEASPOON FRESH LEMON JUICE

2⅓ POUND LAMB SHOULDER, CUT INTO 1½-INCH PIECES

¼ TEASPOON SAFFRON

½ CUP HOT WATER

½ CUP WARM MILK

1 TABLESPOON VEGETABLE OIL

1 MEDIUM ONION, SLICED IN ROUNDELS*

1 CUP ALL-PURPOSE FLOUR

½ CUP WATER

3–4 BAY LEAVES

4 GREEN CARDAMOM PODS

2 ONE-INCH CINNAMON STICKS

¼ TEASPOON WHOLE CLOVES

¼ TEASPOON CARAWAY SEEDS

2 THIN, HOT GREEN CHILE PEPPERS, CUT IN JULIENNE

¼ TEASPOON CORIANDER SEEDS

4 CUPS WHITE BASMATI RICE

3 TABLESPOONS CLARIFIED BUTTER (*GHEE*)†

[Kachhe Gosht ki Biryani, *continued*]

Grind garlic and ginger together into a paste, and set aside. Whip yogurt well with a spoon, and add ½ teaspoon *garam masala,* garlic-ginger paste, cayenne pepper, green chile pepper, half the cilantro and mint leaves, 1 teaspoon salt, papaya, turmeric and lemon juice. Mix well. Marinate the meat in mixture for at least 2–3 hours. Spread marinated meat evenly on the bottom of a large, heavy pot, and set aside. Add saffron to hot water, and blend in warm milk. Set aside.

Heat 1 tablespoon oil in a frying pan over medium heat and sauté onion until uniformly brown and crunchy. Set aside. Mix flour and about ½ cup water to make a puttylike dough to seal the cooking pot. Roll the dough into a tube about an inch thick and long enough to go around the pot. Set aside. Wash and soak rice in enough water to cover for 20–30 minutes. Drain and set aside. Heat 12 cups water in a large pot over high heat. Add 1 teaspoon salt, bay leaves, cardamom, cinnamon stick, cloves, caraway seeds and rest of *garam masala.* When water starts boiling, add chile pepper and coriander seeds. Add rice and stir. After 5 minutes, take out a third of the rice, strain to remove any water and spread over marinated meat. After another 5 minutes, take out half of the rice remaining in the pot and layer it over the previous rice layer. Drain rest of the rice, and layer as before. Pour saffron mixture and clarified butter evenly over rice. To seal pot, place the tube of dough along the rim of the pot. Overlap the ends and discard excess, if any. Cover pot, pressing lid into dough to create a seal. Cook over high heat for 10 minutes, then reduce heat to low and cook 35 minutes more. Garnish with onion and rest of mint and cilantro.

*Cut onion in half vertically, then thinly slice each half at a right angle to cut edge.

†See p. 67 for instructions on making clarified butter. Available at Indian and specialty food markets; also see *Resources,* p. 71, for mail-order suppliers of Indian foods.

Beef Olathu

Stir-fried beef with coconut. Serves 2–3.

The recipe for this dry meat dish was provided by chef P.K. Raju at the Coconut Lagoon Heritage Resort situated on Lake Vembanad in Kumarakom, Kerala.

- 4 WHOLE, SMALL, DRIED, HOT RED CHILE PEPPERS
- 1½ TABLESPOONS CORIANDER SEEDS
- ½ TEASPOON FENNEL SEEDS
- 1 ONE-INCH CINNAMON STICK
- 2 PODS GREEN CARDAMOM
- ¼ TEASPOON TURMERIC
- ½ TABLESPOON BLACK PEPPERCORNS
- 4 TABLESPOONS WATER
- 1 POUND BONELESS, TENDER CHUCK STEAK, CUT IN 1½-INCH CUBES

¼ cup fresh coconut, cut in paper-thin strips

½ tablespoon fresh ginger, cut in julienne

1 thin, hot green chile pepper, finely chopped

6 curry leaves (about ½ sprig)*

½ teaspoon salt

2 teaspoons vinegar

1 medium onion, cut in roundels†

1 tablespoon vegetable oil

Dry roast red chile peppers and coriander seeds for 3–5 minutes over high heat. Remove peppers and set aside. Grind roasted coriander with fennel, cinnamon, cardamom, turmeric and peppercorns in water, making a fine paste. Mix meat with coconut, spice paste, ginger, green chile pepper, curry leaves, salt and vinegar. Cover and cook on medium-low heat for 30 minutes. In a separate pan, sauté onion in oil until golden brown, and add to meat mixture. Crush roasted red chile peppers and stir into meat mixture. Cook, uncovered, for another 30 minutes, or until meat is done and most of the liquid is gone.

*Available at Indian and specialty food markets; also see *Resources,* p. 71, for mail-order suppliers of Indian foods.

†Cut onion in half vertically, then thinly slice each half at a right angle to cut edge.

Balchão

Shrimp marinated in brine sauce. Serves 2–3.

The recipe for this Goan speciality of Portuguese origin was provided by executive chef Julia Carmen de Sa of the Allegria Restaurant in the Taj Exotica Hotel in Goa. It contains shrimp "pickled" in a brine sauce containing sugar, vinegar and spices.

Peri-peri masala (*spice mixture*)

1 garlic clove

1 one-inch piece fresh ginger

¼ teaspoon cumin seeds

1 two-inch stick cinnamon

6 pods green cardamom

8 whole cloves

¼ teaspoon turmeric

½ teaspoon salt

¼ teaspoon black peppercorns

[Balchão, *continued*]

- 4 WHOLE, SMALL, DRIED, HOT RED CHILE PEPPERS, SOAKED OVERNIGHT IN A LITTLE VINEGAR
- 1 TABLESPOON VINEGAR

- 9 OUNCES UNCOOKED SHRIMP WITH TAILS ON
- 2 TABLESPOON VEGETABLE OIL
- 2 CLOVES GARLIC, SLICED
- 1 SPRIG CURRY LEAVES (ABOUT 12 LEAVES)*
- 1 MEDIUM ONION, CUT IN ROUNDELS†
- 1 TEASPOON BROWN SUGAR
- ½ TEASPOON SALT, OR TO TASTE

Grind garlic and ginger together into a paste, and set aside. Finely grind together remaining ingredients of *peri-peri masala* (spice mixture): cumin, cinnamon, cardamom, cloves, turmeric, salt, peppercorns and chile peppers. Mix in garlic-ginger paste and vinegar, and set aside. Sauté shrimp over medium heat in 1 tablespoon of oil until just pink. Remove from heat and set aside. In another pan, heat remaining oil over medium heat. Add sliced garlic, curry leaves and onion. Sauté until onion is golden brown. Add *peri-peri masala* and fry until the vinegar smell goes away. Add sautéed shrimp, brown sugar and salt. Cook for a few minutes more, until heated through.

*Available at Indian and specialty food markets; also see *Resources,* p. 71, for mail-order suppliers of Indian food.

†Cut onion in half vertically, then thinly slice each half at a right angle to cut edge.

Murgh Ka Mokul

Shredded chicken. Serves 2.

This recipe was provided by Sandeep Kalia, executive chef at the Taj Hari Mahal Hotel in Jodhpur, Rajasthan. The dish traditionally was made with rabbit.

- ¾ POUND BONELESS CHICKEN BREAST, CUT INTO SIX PIECES
- 1 TABLESPOON FRESH GINGER, GROUND TO A PASTE (ABOUT A 1-INCH PIECE)
- 2 TABLESPOONS CLARIFIED BUTTER (*GHEE*)* OR BUTTER
- ½ CUP YOGURT, WHISKED TO REMOVE LUMPS
- PINCH SAFFRON
- 3 TABLESPOONS CASHEWS
- 1 TABLESPOON GOLDEN RAISINS

½ TEASPOON SALT, OR TO TASTE

½ TEASPOON WHITE PEPPER

Put chicken in enough boiling water to cover. Reduce heat and simmer for about 15 minutes, or until done. Drain and cool. Shred into small pieces by hand and set aside. In a shallow pan, sauté ginger paste in *ghee* over medium heat for 1 minute. Reduce heat to medium-low and stir in yogurt and saffron. Cook for 3–4 minutes, stirring frequently. Mix in cashews, raisins, salt, pepper and chicken. Cook until chicken is heated through, stirring often.

*See p. 67 for instructions on making clarified butter. Available at Indian and specialty food markets; also see *Resources,* p. 71, for mail-order suppliers of Indian food.

Murgh Tikka Butter Masala

Barbecued chicken in buttery tomato and cream sauce. Serves 3–4.

Chef Sanjay Bhat of the Surabhi Restaurant in Jaipur provided the recipe for this dish of bite-size, marinated chicken pieces, which traditionally are grilled on skewers, *tandoori*-style, in a charcoal-fired oven. Grilled meat is removed from skewers and cooked in a buttery tomato and cream sauce.

Marinade

1½-INCH PIECE FRESH GINGER

2 MEDIUM CLOVES GARLIC

½ CUP WHOLE-MILK YOGURT

1 TABLESPOON LEMON JUICE

1 TABLESPOON MUSTARD OIL*

¼ TABLESPOON *AJWAIN* SEEDS*

1 TEASPOON SALT

1 TEASPOON ORANGE RED POWDER*

2 CUPS BONELESS CHICKEN BREAST, CUT IN 1½-INCH PIECES

VEGETABLE OIL FOR BASTING MARINATED MEAT

¼ CUP UNSALTED BUTTER

½ CUP TOMATO PURÉE

½ CUP WHIPPING CREAM OR CRÉME FRAICHE (RESERVE SOME FOR GARNISH)

½ TEASPOON SALT

PINCH DRY FENUGREEK LEAVES (*KASOORI METHI*)*

½ TEASPOON *GARAM MASALA* (SPECIAL SPICE MIXTURE)*

½ CUP WATER

[Murgh Tikka Butter Masala, *continued*]
Grind garlic and ginger together into a paste, using 1 tablespoon water. Mix 1 tablespoon paste with remaining ingredients of marinade, and marinate chicken overnight in refrigerator. Marinade will be intensely orange.
Next day, skewer chicken and barbecue it over moderate heat, keeping chicken close to, but not touching, grill. Brush with oil as it cooks. Remove chicken from skewers before fully cooked, and set aside.
Heat butter in frying pan over medium to high heat. Add remaining garlic-ginger paste and fry for 3–4 minutes. While stirring constantly, add chicken, tomato purée and most of the cream (reserve about 1 tablespoon for garnish). Stir in salt and fenugreek leaves. Mix well. Add *garam masala* and water. Cook mixture over high heat to boiling. Transfer to a serving dish and garnish with drizzles of cream. Serve with *naan* (leavened flatbread) or rice. See recipe, p. 63.
*Available at Indian and specialty food markets; also see *Resources,* p. 71, for mail-order suppliers of Indian foods.

Bhalolaga Illisher Paturi

Steamed salmon in mustard-yogurt sauce. Serves 4.

Chef Debasish Guha of the Aaheli Restaurant in the Peerless Inn in Kolkata, Bengal, contributed this recipe. It is a very popular and traditional Bengali dish typically made with *illisher* (*hilsa* in Hindi), a fish found in the estuaries of the Bay of Bengal.

4 TABLESPOONS BLACK MUSTARD SEEDS

1 THIN, HOT GREEN CHILE PEPPER, DESEEDED

3 TABLESPOONS WATER

1 TABLESPOON MUSTARD OIL*

1 TEASPOON SALT

½ CUP WHOLE-MILK YOGURT

4 1-INCH THICK SALMON STEAKS (ABOUT 1¾ POUNDS)

BANANA LEAVES

12 WOODEN TOOTHPICKS

Grind mustard seeds, green chile pepper and water together into a paste. Add paste, mustard oil and salt to the yogurt, and mix well. Marinate salmon steaks in the yogurt-mustard paste for 45 minutes. Wash banana leaves and pat dry. Sear leaves to make them more pliable by passing them over a flame several times, being careful not to burn them. Cut leaves in lengths a little longer than twice the width of the steak. Place a marinated steak lengthwise in the middle of each piece of leaf. Bring the sides up over the steak, overlap the edges and hold together with a toothpick. Pinch the ends together and hold with a toothpick. Put wrapped fish in a colander placed over a pot of boiling water; the bottom of the colander should be above the surface of the water. Cover fish with a large pot lid and steam for 20 minutes, or until done. Serve with hot rice.

*Available at Indian and specialty food markets; also see *Resources,* p. 71, for mail-order suppliers of Indian food.

Chingri Malaikari

Shrimp in a rich, red, coconut-milk sauce flavored with garam masala. Serves 2.

The recipe for this dish was contributed by Sadhana Mukherji, a well-known author of several Indian cookbooks, who lives in Kolkata (Calcutta). It is a traditional dish from Bengal typically served with rice pilaf.

1 TABLESPOON CLARIFIED BUTTER (*GHEE*)*

Whole garam masala (*spice mixture*)

1 CINNAMON STICK, BROKEN INTO 1-INCH PIECES

6 GREEN CARDAMOM PODS

½ TEASPOON WHOLE CLOVES

6 TABLESPOONS PURÉED ONION

1 TEASPOON PURÉED FRESH GINGER

1 TEASPOON TURMERIC

¼ TEASPOON CAYENNE PEPPER

2 BAY LEAVES

½ POUND SHRIMP, DEVEINED

1 CUP COCONUT MILK (EXTRACT II) OR ½ CUP CANNED COCONUT MILK AND ½ CUP WATER†

½ TEASPOON SUGAR

⅛ TEASPOON SALT OR TO TASTE

1 CUP COCONUT MILK (EXTRACT I) OR 1 CUP UNDILUTED CANNED COCONUT MILK†

Heat clarified butter in heavy frying pan and fry spice mixture (cinnamon, cardamom and cloves) over medium heat until completely brown. Do not let the *ghee* burn. Add onion, ginger, turmeric, cayenne pepper and bay leaves. Fry until the mixture clumps together and no longer sticks to the pan, about 2–3 minutes. Add shrimp and sauté for a few minutes on medium-high heat. Add coconut milk extract II, sugar and salt. Mix well and cook over high heat until sauce is reduced,

[Chingri Malaikari, *continued*]
about 7 minutes. Add coconut milk extract I and cook for 5–7 minutes. Remove from heat and serve.

*See p. 67 for recipe to prepare clarified butter. Also available at Indian and specialty food markets.

†See p. 68 for instructions to make coconut milk extracts from grated coconut.

Meen Moiley

Fish in creamy coconut sauce. Serves 2–3.

J. Inder Singh (Jiggs) Kalra, India's top culinary expert, celebrated columnist and author, and Pushpesh Pant, noted academic, author and freelance TV producer, provided the recipe for this classic fish dish from the southern state of Kerala. It typically is served with steamed rice.

2 TABLESPOONS VEGETABLE OIL
1 TABLESPOON BLACK MUSTARD SEEDS
1 CLOVE GARLIC, SLIVERED
1-INCH PIECE FRESH GINGER, CUT IN JULIENNE
3 THIN, HOT GREEN CHILE PEPPERS, DESEEDED AND CUT IN JULIENNE
1 MEDIUM ONION, SLICED THINLY INTO ROUNDELS*
¼ TEASPOON TURMERIC
4 FILLETS (1¼ POUNDS) RED SNAPPER, PATTED DRY
¾ CUP COCONUT MILK (EXTRACT III)† OR ¼ CUP CANNED COCONUT MILK AND ½ CUP WATER
SALT TO TASTE
1 SPRIG CURRY LEAVES (ABOUT 12 LEAVES)††
2 MEDIUM TOMATOES, EACH CUT INTO 8 WEDGES
½ CUP COCONUT MILK (EXTRACT II)† OR ¼ CUP CANNED COCONUT MILK AND ¼ CUP WATER
¼–½ CUP COCONUT MILK (EXTRACT I)† OR ¼–½ CUP UNDILUTED CANNED COCONUT MILK
1 TABLESPOON LEMON JUICE

Heat oil in a large frying pan over high heat until shimmering. Add mustard seeds, cover pan and let sputter. When sputtering slows down, reduce heat to medium.

Add garlic and ginger, and stir for one minute. Mix in green chile peppers and stir for another minute. Add onions, and sauté until translucent and glossy. Stir in turmeric, fish and coconut extract III. Bring to a boil, reduce heat to low and simmer for 2–3 minutes, carefully turning fish once. Add salt, curry leaves, tomato and coconut extract II. Cover and simmer for 2–3 minutes, or until fillets are just cooked. Remove pan from stove, uncover and gently stir in coconut extract I so fillets do not break. Return pan to stove and bring to a boil over low heat. Sprinkle with lemon juice and stir carefully. Remove from heat and adjust for seasoning.

*Cut onion in half vertically, then thinly slice each half at a right angle to cut edge.

†See p. 68 for instructions to make coconut milk extracts from grated coconut.

††Available at Indian and specialty food markets; also see *Resources,* p. 71, for mail-order suppliers of Indian food.

Mutton Kolhapuri

Spicy mutton. Serves 4.

The recipe for this dish was contributed by executive chef Hemant Oberoi and chef Vivek Kulkarni of the Taj Mahal Hotel in Mumbai (Bombay). The town of Kolhapur, near Mumbai, is famous for its dried, hot red chile peppers.

½ CUP UNSWEETENED, GRATED, DRIED COCONUT

5 TABLESPOONS VEGETABLE OIL

1 MEDIUM ONION, SLICED

1 TABLESPOON FRESH GINGER, SLICED

4 CLOVES GARLIC, SLICED

4 TABLESPOONS CORIANDER SEEDS

1 TEASPOON WHOLE CLOVES

1 2-INCH CINNAMON STICK

½ TEASPOON ANISE

½ TEASPOON NUTMEG

1 TEASPOON BLACK PEPPERCORNS

½ TEASPOON CUMIN SEEDS

4 WHOLE, SMALL, DRIED, HOT RED CHILE PEPPERS

1 TEASPOON CHOPPED, THIN, HOT GREEN CHILE PEPPER

1 TEASPOON POPPY SEEDS

½ TEASPOON TURMERIC

½ CUP GRATED FRESH COCONUT

1 TEASPOON SALT

[Mutton Kolhapuri, *continued*]

- 2½ CUPS WATER
- 1½ POUND LAMB SHOULDER, CUT IN ONE-INCH CUBES
- 1 SPRIG CURRY LEAVES (ABOUT 12)*
- 4–5 STRIPS THINLY SLICED FRESH COCONUT

Brown dried, grated coconut in a pan over medium heat, and set aside. Heat ¼ cup oil in pan over medium heat. Add onion, ginger and garlic, and fry to a golden color. Transfer to a bowl, keeping as much oil as possible in the pan. To the same pan add coriander, cloves, cinnamon, anise, nutmeg, peppercorns, cumin and red chile peppers. Sauté over medium heat until coriander seeds turn slightly brown, about 2 minutes. Stir in fried onion mixture, green chile peppers, poppy seeds, turmeric, grated, fresh coconut and salt, and cook another 1–2 minutes over medium heat. Grind the mixture to a fine paste with water. Heat 1 tablespoon of oil in a deep frying pan and sauté lamb over medium-high heat for 3–4 minutes. Reduce heat to medium low and cook for 15 minutes. Add ground spice paste. Mix well and adjust for salt. Simmer for another 15 minutes or until meat becomes tender. In a small pan, heat 1 teaspoon of oil over high heat, add curry leaves and sauté for 15 seconds. Garnish the dish with curry leaves and fresh coconut strips.

*Available at Indian and specialty food markets; also see *Resources,* p. 71, for mail-order suppliers of Indian foods.

Chettinad ka Mirch Murga

Chettinad pepper chicken. Serves 4.

The recipe for this dry chicken dish was provided by Meenakshi Meyyappan, a member of the Nattukottai Chettiars, a prosperous banking community in the town of Karaikudi in the Chettinad region of the state of Tamil Nadu. Mrs. Meyyappan has restored her family's weekend home and converted it into a heritage guest house.

- 5 WHOLE, SMALL, DRIED, HOT RED CHILE PEPPERS
- 1 TABLESPOON STAR ANISE
- 4 GARLIC CLOVES
- 1 ONE-INCH PIECE FRESH GINGER
- 2 TABLESPOONS CORIANDER SEEDS
- 1 TABLESPOON FENNEL SEEDS
- 2 TABLESPOONS BLACK PEPPERCORNS
- 1¼ CUPS WATER
- 4 TABLESPOONS VEGETABLE OIL

3 GREEN CARDAMOM PODS

2 WHOLE CLOVES

3 ½-INCH CINNAMON STICKS

2 MEDIUM ONIONS, CHOPPED

½ TEASPOON TURMERIC

2 MEDIUM TOMATOES, CHOPPED

1 WHOLE CHICKEN, CUT INTO 10 PIECES

SALT TO TASTE

Grind red chile peppers, star anise, garlic, ginger, coriander, fennel and peppercorns together in ¼ cup of water, and set aside. Heat oil over medium heat in a heavy pot. Add oil, cardamom, cloves and cinnamon, and stir for 30 seconds. Mix in chopped onion and fry until brown. Add turmeric and spice paste, and cook for a few minutes, stirring frequently. Add tomatoes, chicken, salt and remaining water. Cook on high heat to boiling, then lower heat and simmer, uncovered, until most of the water has evaporated.

BREADS/CRÊPES

Naan

Flat, leavened white bread. Serves 6–8.

The recipe for this ideal accompaniment to meat and *tandoori* dishes was provided by Rajeev Sharma, executive chef at the Samode Palace in the village of Samode, Rajasthan. Now a premier hotel, the palace had been the residence of the princes of the House of Kacchawaha Rajputs.

2 CUPS ALL-PURPOSE FLOUR

¼ TEASPOON SALT

1 TEASPOON BAKING POWDER

¼ TEASPOON BAKING SODA

½ TEASPOON FAST-RISING YEAST

1 EGG, SLIGHTLY BEATEN

1 TEASPOON SUGAR

2 TABLESPOONS WHOLE-MILK YOGURT

½ CUP LUKEWARM WHOLE MILK

3 TABLESPOONS BUTTER

3–4 TABLESPOONS WATER

2 TEASPOONS NIGELLA, FENNEL OR SESAME SEEDS

[Naan, *continued*]

Sift flour with salt, baking powder, soda and yeast. In a separate bowl, whisk egg, sugar, yogurt and milk. Mix butter into flour mixture and add egg mixture. Knead to a soft, smooth dough for about 5 minutes. Add water as needed. Dough should not stick to the fingers when done. Put dough in a bowl and cover with a moist cloth. Set aside in a warm place until dough doubles in size, about 2 hours. Knead dough on a lightly floured surface for a few minutes until smooth. Divide into six to eight equal portions and form balls. Place a ball on floured surface. Roll out slightly, cover and set aside for 5 minutes. Repeat for remaining balls. Flatten each slightly rolled ball, using the palms of the hands or a rolling pin to make a circle about 7 inches in diameter. Pull on one side to form a tear-drop shape and place on ungreased cookie sheet. Sprinkle ¼ teaspoon seeds on each and press gently to embed them in the surface. Bake for 10–15 minutes in a 400°F preheated oven, or until puffy and golden brown on top. Brush surface with butter if desired. Serve hot.

Appam

Fermented rice crêpes. Serves 6–8.

This recipe was contributed by chef Velayudhan (Velu) Koolichalakal of the Spice Village, a member of the Casino Group of hotels in Goa. Traditionally these crêpes are served hot with gravy dishes such as the fish dish *meen moiley* (see recipe, p. 60). Plan ahead: crêpe batter takes three days to prepare.

1¼ CUPS WATER FOR RICE PORRIDGE

½ CUP COARSE WHITE RICE FLOUR

2 CUPS WHITE RICE, SOAKED IN WATER OVERNIGHT*

5–6 CUPS WATER FOR GRINDING RICE AND THINNING BATTER

7 FLUID OUNCES (HALF A CAN) COCONUT MILK

PINCH BAKER'S FAST-RISING YEAST

2 TABLESPOONS SUGAR

1 TEASPOON SALT

VEGETABLE OIL TO GREASE GRIDDLE

Boil water and add rice flour. Reduce heat to low, and cook while stirring for 2–3 minutes. Let the mixture cool. Drain soaked rice and grind in a blender in ½-cup batches, using ½ cup water (more as needed) with each batch to make a fine paste. Add cooked rice, coconut milk, yeast, sugar and salt to the ground rice paste. Mix well to remove lumps. Cover and leave at room temperature overnight. Next day, mix batter well. If lumpy, grind in a blender for a few minutes. Add more water to bring the volume to 5–6 cups. The batter will be thicker than French crêpe batter.

Heat a small wok or a flat griddle over medium heat, add ½ teaspoon vegetable oil and grease the entire surface with a paper towel. Add just under ½ cup batter. If using a wok, spread batter evenly by picking up the wok by the handles and tilting it while gently rotating it in a circle so batter is spread up onto the sides of the wok, reaching 3–4 inches from the bottom. Keep the wok close to the burner while spreading the batter. The sides will have a thin, lacy layer of batter; the bottom will have a thicker layer. If using a flat griddle, make similar movements to spread the batter evenly. Cover and cook for 2–3 minutes, or until the edges are golden. Crêpes will be about 8 inches in diameter. Those cooked in a wok will not be flat and will be thicker in the middle.

*Use any long grain rice variety except a fragrant one such as Basmati or jasmine.

Desserts

Sheer Khurma

Vermicelli sweet. Serves 3–4.

This recipe was provided by Sahebzade Syeda Uzma Khan, daughter of the heir-apparent to the present Nawab of Sheesh Mahal in Lucknow. Popular throughout India, this dish has many regional variations. The southern version, a much thinner mixture containing coconut, is called *payasam.*

- ¼ CUP CASHEW PIECES
- ¼ CUP BLANCHED AND SLIVERED ALMONDS
- 4 CUPS WHOLE MILK
- ¼ CUP ROASTED INDIAN OR PAKISTANI VERMICELLI*
- ¼ CUP SUGAR
- ½ CUP DATES, CHOPPED INTO SMALL PIECES
- 1 PIECE EDIBLE SILVER FOIL (*VARQ*) ABOUT 3 INCHES SQUARE, TORN INTO FOUR PIECES (OPTIONAL)†

Combine nuts and fry without butter over low heat until lightly toasted. Remove from pan and set aside. In a heavy saucepan, bring milk to a boil over high heat, stirring constantly. Reduce heat to medium, add vermicelli and cook until the volume is reduced by half, about 30 minutes, stirring frequently. Add sugar, nuts and dates, mixing well. Cook for a few minutes more. Transfer to individual bowls and place a piece of silver foil on top. Serve hot or chilled.

*Available at Indian and specialty food markets and many organic food stores; also see *Resources,* p. 71, for mail-order suppliers of Indian food. Do not substitute with the much thicker, Italian-style vermicelli. Note that roasted Indian or Pakistani vermicelli products can vary somewhat in color. If the product purchased is not golden brown, carefully sauté it in a small amount of butter (⅛–¼ teaspoon) over low heat until it is golden brown; cool. If the vermicelli is not in short pieces, break into pieces about 1 inch in length.

†See *Resources,* p. 71, for mail-order suppliers of Indian foods.

Beverages

Sambaram

Savory cultured milk drink. Serves 4.

This recipe was provided by the culinary staff of Spice Coast Cruises, which is operated by the Coconut Lagoon Resort in Kumarakom, Kerala. Passengers ride on long cargo boats (*kettuvallam*) that have been converted into houseboats and are treated to preparations of local cuisine as they lazily cruise through the backwaters of Kerala.

6 CUPS PLAIN CULTURED MILK*

6 CURRY LEAVES†

½ TEASPOON SALT

2 TABLESPOONS GRATED FRESH GINGER

2 THIN, HOT GREEN CHILE PEPPERS, DESEEDED AND FINELY CHOPPED

8 SHALLOTS, CHOPPED

¼ TEASPOON CUMIN SEEDS, COARSELY GROUND

1 LIME, CUT INTO WEDGES

In a large bowl, mix all ingredients except lime. Let stand for 15 minutes. Strain mixture, using a spoon to press the solids to extract the flavor. Mix well and serve chilled with a lime wedge.

*Can substitute whole-milk yogurt diluted with water (1 cup yogurt to ½ cup water, or to desired consistency).

†Available at Indian and specialty food markets; also see *Resources,* p. 71, for mail-order suppliers of Indian foods.

Masala Chai

Spicy tea. Serves 2.

This recipe was provided by Indumati Menon, who lives in New Delhi.

Tea masala (*tea spice mixture, bulk recipe*)*

12 BLACK CARDAMOM PODS

26 GREEN CARDAMOM PODS

1½ TABLESPOONS WHOLE BLACK PEPPERCORNS

1 TABLESPOON WHOLE CLOVES

1 TEASPOON GROUND CINNAMON

¾ CUP POWDERED DRIED GINGER

1 CUP WHOLE MILK

1 CUP WATER

½ TEASPOON TEA *MASALA*

4 TEASPOONS SUGAR, OR TO TASTE

2 TEASPOONS TEA LEAVES (PREFERABLY ASSAM TEA)

Grind cardamom, peppercorns and cloves to a powder. Add to cinnamon and ginger, and mix well. If desired, adjust the amount of spices to suit your taste after trying this recipe. Store in an air-tight container and use as needed in recipe above.

In a saucepan bring milk, water, tea *masala* and sugar to a boil. Add tea leaves and reduce heat. Simmer for 5 minutes or longer, depending on the desired color of tea. Remove from burner, cover and steep for a few minutes. Pour tea through a strainer into cups. Drink hot.

*Makes 1 cup.

MISCELLANEOUS

Ghee

Clarified butter. Makes about 1½ cups.

1 LB UNSALTED BUTTER

Melt butter over medium heat in a heavy saucepan; reduce heat to low. Cook for about 30 minutes or until there is a brown film on the bottom of the pan and the liquid butter is clear. Do not let it become brown. Allow to cool but not solidify. Slowly pour the liquid into a screw-cap jar through a small tea strainer lined with a coffee filter. Tightly close jar and refrigerate. Keeps for three months or longer if all the milk solids have been removed. Discard rancid-smelling *ghee.*

Paneer

Indian farmer's cheese. Makes 1½ cups (about 12 ounces).

8 CUPS WHOLE MILK

½ CUP WHITE VINEGAR

CHEESECLOTH

Bring milk to a boil and add vinegar while stirring. The milk will curdle and separate into curds and whey. Pour the curdled milk into a colander lined with cheesecloth. Gather cloth around the freshly made curds, and squeeze gently to

[Paneer, *continued*]

remove excess whey. Rinse with water and squeeze gently. Place cheese and cloth on a bread board. Spread cloth over the surface of the board and move cheese to one end. Shape cheese into a 7-inch square and cover with the rest of the cloth. Prop the board so it is slanted. Put another bread board on the cheese and top with a weight. This will compress the cheese and help squeeze out the whey, which will drain away down the slanted board. After 3–4 hours, remove weight and slide flattened, compacted cheese onto a plate. Cut into pieces of desired size.

Coconut Milk

It is easy to make coconut milk from freshly grated coconut and capture the authentic taste of Indian dishes using it. A thick, rich milk is produced from the first squeezing of the gratings; thinner milks are derived from a second and third round of squeezing.

1 COCONUT*

½ CUP WARM WATER (FOR THICK MILK, EXTRACT I)

2 CUPS WARM WATER (FOR THIN MILK, EXTRACTS II & III)

Heat the coconut in a preheated oven (350°F) for 10 minutes. Cracks will form in the coconut. Remove it from the oven (with potholders!) and place in a large metal bowl on the floor. Cover the bowl with a towel and hit the coconut with a hammer to break it completely open. More than one strike may be necessary. Remove the pieces of broken coconut from the bowl. Strain the coconut water that is released through a coffee filter to remove any fibers, and set aside. Separate the coconut meat from the shell, using a dull knife to pry them apart if necessary. Remove the brown skin from the coconut meat with a vegetable peeler and grate the meat in a food processor.

To make the thick milk (extract I), put the gratings into cheesecloth or a clean white dish towel and hold the ends together. Soak the wrapped gratings in ½ cup warm water in a small bowl for a few minutes. Firmly squeeze the gratings over the bowl. About ¾ cup of thick milk will be obtained.

Thinner milk (extract II) is made by soaking the same wrapped gratings in 1 cup warm water and repeating the squeezing procedure. Use the reserved coconut water to bring the volume to 1 cup, if necessary. Repeat once more to generate extract III.

*Before buying a coconut, shake it to make sure it contains water.

Shopping in India's Food Markets

Helpful Tips

Outdoor Markets

Travelers to India intent on exploring the lively outdoor markets will learn more about the food and gain valuable insight into Indian culture. Nothing brings strangers together more pleasantly than food, and India's villages and cities all told have a multitude of marketplaces with copious fresh produce and cheery vendors to make such encounters almost certain.

We favor the large rural weekly markets. There is a tangible, heightened level of excitement between vendors as they enjoy catching up on gossip with each other between sales. Vendors place their edibles in eye-catching colorful groupings to make purchasing them irresistible. Food is priced, but often not named. If you don't recognize something, be prepared to ask, "What is this called?" (see *Helpful Phrases,* p. 75). If you intend to buy, don't expect much haggling over the price. It is unlikely you will find cheaper prices or fresher food anywhere. Usually thrown in with a vegetable purchase is an appreciated freebie: a small bunch of cilantro and some fresh green chile peppers. Meat for sale is from animals butchered on market day, necessitated by the lack of refrigeration. Chickens often are slaughterd at the time of purchase. The multi-colored, free-running fowl are highly regarded and bring a higher price. In coastal areas fishmongers hawk the catch of the day. The tangy smell of the sea is tossed in at no extra cost. A variety of non-food items will be found in another section of the market.

Smaller open markets operating daily include neighborhood stores and the many mobile and stationary carts of street vendors. There also are specialty stores selling only one type of food, such as fruits or vegetables. Fruit markets usually are located right next to ones selling vegetables. Smaller markets have higher prices and a reduced selection.

So many images in the markets beg for photographic capture. Some folks however, are reticent about having their picture taken. Always ask first.

The Indoor Markets

Food sold indoors is more expensive. Stores range from small neighborhood convenience shops to supermarkets—a more recent phenomenon—with a wide assortment of groceries and non-comestibles. You may be tempted to get the makings for a tasty picnic. Remember to pack some lightweight tableware before leaving home!

The following abbreviated list of weights in transliterated Hindi proved sufficient to get the quantities we wanted. Corresponding approximate weights in pounds are included.

sau gram: 100 grams, or about ¼ pound
dhai sau gram: 250 grams, or about ½ pound
adha kilo: half kilo, or about 1 pound

If you are considering bringing food back to the United States, obtain the USDA-APHIS brochure "Travelers' Tips" beforehand to see which items are allowed. It is available online at www.aphis.usda.gov/travel/usdatips.html or by writing to:

USDA-APHIS "Travelers' Tips" Brochure #1083
Plant Protection & Quarantine / Marketing & Regulatory Programs
4700 River Road, Unit 133
Riverdale, MD 20737

A Health Precaution

Don't ask for trouble. Some serious diseases can be transmitted by eating unclean produce. If you buy fruits and vegetables in the markets, make sure to wash them thoroughly before eating. The safest fruits are those that can be peeled. Avoid eating food from street vendors. Bottled water is readily available and is a wise choice, even in restaurants.

Resources

Mail-Order Suppliers of Indian Food Items

Many retail sources sell the special ingredients required for the recipes in this book. These ingredients are available in Indian food markets, other ethnic grocery stores such as Asian Markets, natural and whole food stores, and large supermarkets. Good sources of fresh or (more likely) frozen banana leaves are Asian and Latino markets.

Several mail-order suppliers of Indian foods are listed below. Most of these stores do not have a catalog, but many carry most or all of the ingredients used in the recipes and will ship them to you. Please let us know if you discover that any of these stores has gone out of business since this book was printed.

Indian food items also can be purchased online from several websites. An example is indiaplaza.com/grocery/groceries. A list of Indian grocery stores is found at sholay.com/food/grocery1.htm. Since websites change or often are not updated with regularity, you will probably need to do additional browsing. We suggest that you use your favorite search engine (our standby is google.com) and do a general search for Indian food markets or a specific search for a certain ingredient.

Kalustyan's
123 Lexington Ave.
New York, NY 10016
Tel: 212-685-3451
Tel: 800-352-3451
Fax: 212-683-8458
www.kalustyans.com
sales@kalustyans.com

Little India Food Market
5766 Evers Rd.
San Antonio, TX 78238
Tel/Fax: 210-521-4778
rpsjuneja@hotmail.com

Bombay Emporium
294 Craft Ave.
Pittsburgh, PA 15213
Tel: 412-682-4965

Indian Grocery Store
2342 Douglas Rd.
Coral Gables, FL 33134
Tel/Fax: 305-448-5869

Beryl's Cake Decorating Supplies
PO Box 1584
North Springfield, VA 22151
Tel: 800-488-2749
Fax: 703-750-3779
www.beryls.com
beryls@beryls.com (request catalog)
Reliable source of edible silver foil (*varq*)

Tours and Travel Agencies

We heartily recommend Travel Scope, an agency in New Delhi, for all your travel needs in India. P. N. Narayanaswamy (Mohan) and Shoba Mohan, owners of Travel Scope, pulled together an itinerary that fulfilled all of our needs perfectly. Our accommodations were most satisfactory, and our guides were top-notch. They were chosen because they were experienced in the topic of greatest interest to us, Indian food. Because we were so pleased with the service provided by Travel Scope, we have partnered with them to lead culinary tours to India. For more information or to request a flyer, send an email message to Joan Peterson at info@ginkgopress.com. We hope you'll want to join us in getting to the heart of the culture through an exploration of India's delicious cuisine! Of course, we'll also see the major tourist sights and still have time to shop and relax along the way.

Contact: Mohan Narayanaswamy
Travel Scope (India) Private Limited
C-58, Malviya Nagar
New Delhi - 11 00 16
Tel: 91 (11) 26687593, 26680895
Fax: 91 (11) 26683979
www.travelscopeindia.com
travelscope@vsnl.com

Some Useful Organizations to Know About

Indian Tourism Office

3550 Wilshire Blvd., Rm 204
Los Angeles, CA 90010
Tel: 213-380-8855
Fax: 213-380-6111
www.tourismofindia.com

Consulate General of India

Chicago:
455 N. City Front Plaza Dr.
(NBC Tower Bldg.) Suite 850
Chicago, IL 60611
Tel: 312-595-0405
Fax: 312-595-0417/18
www.IndianConsulate.com

New York:
3 East 64th St.
New York, NY 10021
Tel: 212-774-0600
Fax: 212-861-3788
www.Indiacgny.org

International Organizations

We are members of two international organizations that promote good will and understanding between people of different cultures. These organizations, Servas and The Friendship Force, share similar ideals but operate somewhat differently.

Servas

Servas, from the Esperanto word meaning "serve," is a non-profit system of travelers and hosts. Servas members travel independently and make their own contacts with fellow members in other countries, choosing hosts with attributes of interest from membership rosters. It is a wonderful way to get to know people, be invited into their homes as a family member, share experiences and help promote world peace. For more information about membership in Servas, write or call:

US Servas Committee, Inc.
11 John St., Room 505
New York, NY 10038
Tel: 212-267-0252
Fax: 212-267-0292
www.usservas.org
info@usservas.org

The Friendship Force

The Friendship Force is a non-profit organization that also fosters good will through encounters between people of different backgrounds. Unlike Servas, Friendship Force members travel in groups to host countries. Both itinerary and travel arrangements are made by a member acting as exchange director. These trips combine stays with a host family and group travel within the host country. For more information on membership in The Friendship Force, write:

The Friendship Force
34 Peachtree St., Suite 900
Atlanta, GA 30303
Tel: 404-522-9490
Fax: 404-688-6148
info@friendshipforce.org
www.friendshipforce.org

Helpful Phrases

For Use in Restaurants and Food Markets

In the Restaurant

These transliterated Hindi phrases help you order food, learn about dishes you order, and determine what regional specialties are available. To help pronounce each transliteration, a phonetic interpretation is written below it. Syllables in capital letters are accented. A circumflex over the letter a (ă) denotes its sound in the word hat. Words ending with a slight "n" sound have (n) written after their last letter. Gender is denoted by (m), masculine; (f), feminine.

DO YOU HAVE A MENU?	Aap ke pas menu hai? *Ahp keh pahs* menu *hă?*
MAY I SEE THE MENU?	Kya mai menu dekh sakhthi (f) / sakhtha (m) hu? *Kee-YAH mă* menu *dake SUHK-tee (f) / SUHK-tah (m) hoo?*
WHAT DO YOU RECOMMEND? (WHAT'S GOOD?)	Aap ka kya sujhav hai? *Ahp kah kee-YAH SOO-jahv hă?*
DO YOU HAVE . . . HERE? (ADD AN ITEM FROM THE *MENU GUIDE* OR THE *FOODS & FLAVORS GUIDE*.)	Kya yaha . . . mil sakhtha hai? *Kee-YAH yah-HAH . . . mill SUHK-tah hă?*

WHAT IS THE "SPECIAL" FOR TODAY? (WHAT'S GOOD TODAY?)	Aajki kya cheez khas hai? *AHDG-kee kee-YAH cheez kahs hă?*
DO YOU HAVE ANY SPECIAL REGIONAL DISHES?	Kya koi ees elaiki ki khas cheez hai? *Kee-YAH KOH-ee iss ee-LEYE-keh kee kahs cheez hă?*
IS THIS DISH SPICY/HOT?	Kya ye cheez mirchi ki hai? *Kee-YAH yeh cheez MEER-chee kee hă?*
I/WE WOULD LIKE TO ORDER . . .	Mai / hum lainge . . . *Mă / hum LENG-gay . . .*
WHAT ARE THE INGREDIENTS IN THIS DISH? (WHAT IS IN THIS DISH?)	Ees me kya-kya cheez hai? *Iss may kee-YAH-kee-YAH cheez hă?*
WHAT ARE THE SEASONINGS IN THIS DISH?	Ees me kon se masale hai? *Iss may kawn say mah-SAH-lay hă?*
THANK YOU VERY MUCH. THE FOOD IS (VERY) DELICIOUS.	Bhuat shukaryeeya. Khana (bhuat) acha hai. *Bah-HOOT shoo-KREE-yah. KAH-nah (bah-HOOT) AH-chah hă.*

In the Market

The following phrases will help you make purchases and learn more about unfamiliar produce, spices and herbs.

WHAT ARE THE REGIONAL FRUITS AND VEGETABLES?	Ees elaike ke kohn si sabzi aur fal hai? *Iss ee-LEYE-keh kay kawn see SUB-zee or fahl hă?*
WHAT IS THIS CALLED?	Ees ko kya khate hai? *Iss koh kee-YAH KAT-teh hă?*
DO YOU HAVE . . . HERE? (ADD AN ITEM FROM THE *FOODS & FLAVORS GUIDE.*)	Kya . . . mile ga? *Kee-YAH . . . MILL-eh gah?*
MAY I TASTE THIS?	Kya mai ess koh chuckh sakhthi (f) / sakhtha (m) hu? *Kee-YAH mă iss kaw(n) chuck SUHK-tee (f) / SUHK-tah (m) who(n)?*
WHERE CAN I BUY FRESH . . . ?	Kha yeh taza mil sakhtha hai . . . ? *Kah yeh TAH-zah mill SUHK-tah hă . . . ?*
HOW MUCH IS THIS PER KILOGRAM (KG)?	Yeh ek kilo keytnay ka hai? *Yeh ake KEE-loh kitten-NAY kah hă?*
I WOULD LIKE TO BUY ½ KILOGRAM (KG) OF THIS.	Mujhe yeh adha kilo dehdho. *MOO-jay yeh ah-DHA KEE-loh DEH-doh.*
MAY I PHOTOGRAPH THIS?	Kya mai eska foto lehloo? *Kee-YAH mă ISS-kah FO-to LAY-loo?*

Other Useful Phrases

It helps to see a transliterated Hindi word or phrase in writing. The following phrase is handy if you want to see what you are hearing.

PLEASE WRITE IT ON THE PAPER.	Esko kagaz per likh dho. *ISS-koh KAH-gahdg per lick doh.*

Interested in bringing home books about Indian food?

WHERE CAN I BUY AN INDIAN COOKBOOK IN ENGLISH?	Moojhay kahnah bananay ki kitab angrayji mai kaha melagi? *Moo-JAY kah-nah bah-nah-NEH kee kee-TAHB uhng-RAY-jee mă kah-HAH mel-ay-GHEE?*

And, of course, the following phrases also are useful to know.

WHERE IS THE RESTROOM?	Toilets kha hai? *Toilets kah hă?*
MAY I HAVE THE BILL?	Kerpya bill dehdho? *KEER-pee-yah bill DEH-doh?*
DO YOU ACCEPT CREDIT CARDS? TRAVELERS CHECKS?	Credit cards / travelers checks le the hai? *Credit cards / travelers checks lay tay hă?*

TOP LEFT Betel leaf packet (*paan*) decorated with silver foil. **TOP RIGHT** *Meen moiley,* southern Indian dish of fish in creamy coconut sauce. **MIDDLE** Southern Indian crêpe (*dosa*) and steamed "cakes" (*idli*) made with rice and lentils, with sauces and chutneys, served at Sagar Restaurant, New Delhi. **BOTTOM** *Achariya aloo,* western Indian dish of "pickled" potatoes made at the Karni Bhawan Hotel in Jodhpur, Rajasthan.

TOP LEFT Chef Raminder Malhotra, Mercurries Restaurant, New Delhi, with a house specialty, kebab of chicken. **TOP RIGHT** Chef J.P. Singh, Bukhara Restaurant, Maurya Sheraton in New Delhi, with a medley of grilled dishes from the Northwest Frontier. **BOTTOM** Popular snack (*chaat*) made with potatoes and chickpeas topped with yogurt, pomegranate seeds, coriander sauce and tamarind sauce.

TOP LEFT The two spice treasures of the nutmeg fruit: nutmeg within the dark shell of the seed, and mace, the red sheath surrounding the seed. **TOP RIGHT** Stacked disk-shaped sweets (*phirni*), a popular Rajasthani treat made of fine threads of dough. **MIDDLE** Orderly market display of dried beans, lentils and chickpeas. **BOTTOM** Watery rose apple, or water apple, whose crispy, juicy flesh is a good thirst quencher.

TOP Bengali version of the traditional "plate" meal (*thali*) served in little bowls (*katoris*) on a metal plate, also called a *thali,* at the Aaheli Restaurant, Kolkata, West Bengal. **MIDDLE** Contemporary version of a *thali* served in crockery, featured at the Masala Art Restaurant in the Taj Palace Hotel, New Delhi. **BOTTOM** *Galawat kabab,* papaya-tenderized fried lamb patties served at the Taj Residency Hotel in Lucknow, Uttar Pradesh.

TOP LEFT Young fishmongers in the outdoor market in Tellicherry, Kerala. **TOP RIGHT** Friendly vegetable seller in the wholesale market in Hyderabad, Andhra Pradesh. **BOTTOM** Stall featuring the foods of the state of Rajasthan, in Dilli Haat, an open air market in New Delhi.

TOP Sampler of famous West Bengali sweets made with milk products. **MIDDLE** *Lal maas,* red lamb stew, with a spicy yogurt gravy rich in red chile peppers. Traditionally, the rich red coloring of this favorite lamb dish of Rajasthan is produced with *rattanjog,* a natural dye made from the cinnamon-like bark of a Kashmiri tree. **BOTTOM** Popular southern Indian snack of fried, donut-shaped rice "cakes" (*vada*) eaten with coconut chutney and a spicy broth (*rasam*), served at the Sagar Restaurant, New Delhi.

TOP LEFT Colorful display of spices sold in the weekly Mapusa Market in Goa. **TOP RIGHT** Vendor selling shaved ice topped with flavored syrups in Jodhpur, Rajasthan. **BOTTOM** Exuberant vegetable seller in the Shoba Bazaar in Kolkata, West Bengal.

TOP LEFT Whole coconut stuffed with shrimp, served at Kewpie's Restaurant, Kolkata, West Bengal. **MIDDLE LEFT** *Nibu chaval,* a southern Indian dish of rice flavored with lemon and spices. **RIGHT** *Chakka* (jackfruit), helfy, tree-borne fruits, which can grow to 80 pounds. **BOTTOM** Specialties of Rajasthan, including *kair kadh* (on the right), a spicy vegetable dish containing a wild, berry-like desert survival food called *kair,* served at the Taj Hari Mahal, Jodhpur, Rajasthan.

Menu Guide

This alphabetical listing is an extensive compilation of menu entries in transliterated Hindi, with English translations to help make ordering food easier. About fifty percent of the population speak Hindi as their primary language. Since you will encounter more than one spelling of transliterated words on menus and elsewhere, we have cross referenced certain spelling variations for some words. If you have difficulty finding a word in this *Guide,* try spelling it phonetically to see the possible alternatives. Following modern convention, diacritical marks and accents were omitted in the transliterations.

The *Menu Guide* has typical Indian dishes as well as special regional ones. While it was not feasible to list each entry in the many different languages spoken in India besides Hindi, the local name of a regional dish in a non-Hindi-speaking area or state was used.

It probably will appear strange at first to see that some of the entries are in English or include English words in their name. This is the result of more than 300 years of British rule. India gained her independence from Britain in 1947. Nevertheless, English is widely understood in urban centers, and is still used for many official purposes.

Classic regional dishes of India that should not be missed are labeled "regional classic" in the margin next to the menu entry. Some noteworthy dishes popular throughout much of the country—also not to be missed—are labeled "national favorite." Of course, some regional classics are national favorites as well. Comments on some of our favorites also are included in the margin.

Not surprisingly, Indian restaurants range from small neighborhood eateries to upscale establishments in prestigious hotels. Some small restaurants are called hotels because the locals associate eating with this word.

Indians begin their day with breakfast (*nashta*) around 9 or 10 AM. A late-morning snack is enjoyed around 11 AM or 12 noon. Lunch (*dopahar ka khana*) is served around 1 or 2 PM. Tea time (*chaipan*) is 4 or 5 PM. Dinner (*rat ka khana*) begins about 8 or 9 PM.

NATIONAL FAVORITE **aam ka achar** mango pickle.

aam ki chutni sweet mango chutney.

DELICIOUS **aam ki lassi** mango yogurt drink.

aam ras mango juice.

aamti spicy dish from the state of Maharashtra made with a variety of split yellow lentils (*toor dal*).

achariya aloo "pickled" potatoes. See recipe, p. 44.

REGIONAL CLASSIC **ada payasam** milk-based dessert containing bits of steamed rice flour paste. Also called *ada pradhaman*.

ajwaini jhinga shrimp marinated in yogurt and spices and seasoned with *ajwain* (bishop's weed), small, ridged, brownish-green seeds that taste like a pungent type of thyme.

REGIONAL CLASSIC **akuri** spicy Parsi dish of soft scrambled eggs with onions, tomatoes, chile peppers and cilantro. Also spelled *ekoori*.

alebele Goan pancake filled with a spiced coconut mixture.

alisi crêpe made from ground rice and a type of lentil (*urad dal*), which is topped with a shredded meat mixture and rolled up like a jellyroll. Two sides of the circle are folded to the center before rolling to help keep the contents from spilling out. The roll is then fried in a little vegetable oil. It is a traditional starter dish in the Mopillah Muslim community of northern Kerala. Also called *omanapura*.

REGIONAL CLASSIC **aloo Banarasi** small, whole, fried potatoes in a spicy, yogurt-based gravy with cilantro and tamarind. The name Banarasi refers to the sacred Hindu city of Banaras (Varanasi) on the banks of the Ganges in the state of Uttar Pradesh.

aloo bhaja fried potato slices or sticks, often flavored with turmeric.

REGIONAL CLASSIC **aloo bonda** fried ball of mashed potatoes. It is a southern Indian snack.

aloo kachori small, deep-fried bread filled with a savory potato mixture.

aloo makalla deep-fried potatoes with tomatoes, flavored with ginger, cayenne, green chile peppers and *ajwain* (bishop's weed). Piquancy is provided by powdered dried mango or pomegranate seeds.

aloo methi northern Indian dish of diced potatoes fried with fresh fenugreek leaves, flavored with turmeric, cumin and cayenne pepper.

aloo palak paratha *paratha* (type of fried, flatbread) stuffed with spicy mashed potatoes mixed with finely chopped spinach. It is griddle-fried in clarified butter or oil.

aloo paratha *paratha* (type of fried, flatbread) stuffed with spicy mashed potatoes and griddle-fried in clarified butter or oil. *Paratha* filled with potatoes is very popular in India. NATIONAL FAVORITE

aloo peper (pepey) dalna Bengali curried dish of diced potato and green papaya.

aloo raita potatoes in a spicy yogurt sauce.

aloo shak dry Gujarati dish of potatoes stir-fried in spices and a little oil.

amb halad ka achaar hot-and-sour pickle made with zedoary, a turmeric-like rhizome.

amb halad ka shorba type of vegetable soup made with zedoary, a turmeric-like rhizome.

ambot tik (amotik) Goan hot-and-sour fish dish.

amiri pulao rich Punjabi rice dish with raisins, figs and bayleaf.

amrakhand chilled dessert made with fresh yogurt, mashed farmers' cheese, mango purée and sweetened condensed milk. REGIONAL CLASSIC

ananas sassam pineapple curry. See recipe, p. 43.

ande ki bhorji scrambled eggs with cumin and sautéed onions.

appam crêpe made of rice and coconut milk. Cooked in a round-bottomed pan, the crêpe has thin, lacy sides and a thicker bottom. Traditionally it is served hot with gravy dishes. See recipe, p. 64. REGIONAL CLASSIC

arisalu (ariselu) crispy fried cookie made of powdered, roasted rice and a thick syrup made of raw sugar from palm or sugar cane juice. It is a popular treat in Andhra Pradesh.

ashrafi coin-shaped sweet made of almond paste and thickened milk, flavored with saffron. A small ball of dough is pressed between two gold coins and bears their inscription. It is a specialty of Hyderabad. REGIONAL CLASSIC

avakai thoku fiery-hot mango pickle, a specialty of Hyderabad.

avial southern Indian dish containing several vegetables, cut in uniform 1-inch pieces, in yogurt and coconut sauce. Potatoes, yams, carrots, gourds, plaintains, jackfruit, green beans and drumsticks, the green pods of the Indian horseradish tree, typically are used. See recipe, p. 47. REGIONAL CLASSIC

badam halwa almond halva, a fudge-like almond sweet. REGIONAL CLASSIC

badam ki jaali sandwich cookie with serrated edges, filled with sweetened almond paste. The filling can be seen through small holes in the cookie layers. It is a Hyderabadi sweet.

baingan bharta baked or charcoal-roasted eggplant, puréed and mixed with tomato, onion and spices. NATIONAL FAVORITE

bajra roti griddle-fried, round, flatbread made of millet flour.

balchão Goan dish of Portuguese origin containing meat, seafood or fish marinated in a sweet, vinegary paste of spices. See recipe for *balchão* made with shrimp, p. 55.

NATIONAL FAVORITE **bara kabab** lamb chops or rack of lamb marinated in yogurt and spices. It is a northern Indian specialty.

batata poha spicy western Indian dish of diced potatoes and flattened rice eaten for breakfast or as a snack.

batata talasani snack of julienne potatoes fried in spices.

REGIONAL CLASSIC **batata vada** fritters made from a spicy mashed potato mixture. Small balls are flattened, coated with batter made from the flour of a lentil called *chana dal* and deep-fried until golden brown. It is a popular street snack in the state of Maharashtra.

batloo flat, griddle-fried bread of Gujarat made with millet flour.

REGIONAL CLASSIC **batti** very dense, small, round roll made from whole-wheat flour dough. When baked, the roll is pressed on top to crack open its crust, and melted clarified butter is ladled over it. It is a specialty of Rajasthan. See *dal batti churma,* this *Guide*.

battia griddle-cooked thin wheat bread with pinch marks on its surface, which are made by the fingers while the bread is cooking. When almost done, it is removed from the griddle and held over a flame to form little black spots on the surface. The bread is then crumpled by gentle squeezing and topped with melted, freshly churned butter. It is a specialty of Rajasthan.

YUMMY **bean poriyal** green beans with coconut. See recipe, p. 47.

beef olathu stir-fried beef with coconut. See recipe, p. 54.

beet khuta sweet and sour curried chicken with beets. It is a dish associated with the once-thriving Cochini Jewish community in the state of Kerala.

bekti jhol *bekti,* a popular Bengali fish with boneless flesh, stewed with potatoes, pointed gourd and green bananas in a spicy, thin gravy flavored with cilantro.

Bengali khatta mitha chana dal sweet-and-sour Bengali lentil dish made with *chana dal.* It is a thick mixture of cooked lentils sweetened with sugar and drizzled with a Bengali spice mix called *panch phoron,* which contains black mustard seeds, fennel seeds, fenugreek seeds, cumin seeds and black caraway seeds.

NATIONAL FAVORITE **besan ke ladoo** small, sweet cardamom-flavored balls made of chickpea flour.

besan thepla soft, flat, griddle-cooked bread made from chickpea flour, wheat flour and millet flour mixed with spices, herbs and yogurt. It is a regional specialty of western Gujarat.

bhagare baingan dish of fried eggplant with onions, green chile peppers and garlic, flavored with coriander, turmeric, *garam masala*, coconut and tamarind.

bhaja baingan Bengali dish of eggplant coated in chickpea flour and deep-fried until crispy.

bhajia (bhajiya) savory, fritter-like snack of sliced vegetables, especially onions, coated in seasoned chickpea batter and deep-fried. Also called *pakora*. NATIONAL FAVORITE

bhalolaga illisher paturi Bengali fish dish made with *illisher,* a popular fish found in the estuaries of the Bay of Bengal. The fish, called *hilsa* in Hindi, is marinated in mustard oil and spices, wrapped in banana leaves and steamed. The mustardy, oily sauce produced in the cooking process is served with rice. Also called *paturi mach*. See recipe, p. 58. REGIONAL CLASSIC

bhape chingri Bengali dish of steamed shrimp.

bharani soup chicken soup flavored with crushed pepper, a traditional dish of the Syrian Christians in Kerala.

bharwa(n) baingan stuffed eggplant dish.

bhatura puffy, round, deep-fried leavened bread made from all-purpose flour, yogurt and clarified butter. Semolina sometimes is added to the dough. This Punjabi specialty commonly is served with chickpeas. NATIONAL FAVORITE

bheeda per eda Parsi dish of okra with eggs.

bhel (bel) puri street snack containing puffed rice, thin wafers made of lentils, deep-fried vermicelli, potatoes, onions, raw mango and various chutneys. It is the most common street food in Mumbai (Bombay). REGIONAL CLASSIC

bhindana bhajiya savory, fritter-like snack of okra coated in seasoned chickpea batter and deep-fried.

bhindi mappas okra stew.

bhoona khichri dish of stir-fried lentils and rice.

bhooni hui simla mirch dish of stir-fried green bell peppers.

bhutte ka kabab fried corn and mint patty.

biryani elaborate dish made with lamb, chicken, vegetables, or even fish, cooked with saffron-flavored rice. Marinated meat (or vegetables and fish) is placed at the bottom of a heavy pot and topped with several layers of partially cooked rice. Each layer of rice added to the pot is less cooked than the layer on top of it. This ensures that all rice is cooked to the same extent when the dish is done, because the rice closer to the bottom of the pot cooks more quickly. The pot and lid are sealed with a putty-like strip of dough, and the pot's contents are steamed in ELEGANT their own juices. Traditionally, hot coals are placed on the pot lid to help the dish cook uniformly.

REGIONAL CLASSIC **bisibella bath** rice and lentil dish with mixed vegetables, red chile peppers, mustard seeds and lemon juice. It is a specialty of Karnataka.

bombil ambotic vinegary, spicy Goan fish dish made with Bombay duck, a marine lizard fish abundant in the seas around the islands comprising the city of Mumbai (Bombay).

bondas savory snack made with deep-fried chickpea batter. See *bhajia,* this *Guide.*

FABULOUS **boondi ladoo** round sweet made from deep-fried chickpea flour droplets and other ingredients such as nuts and raisins, which is eaten at special events and parties. It is a treat found in sweet shops; also simply called *ladoo.*

boondi raita yogurt with deep-fried chickpea flour pearls (*boondi ladoo*).

boti kababs Moghlai dish of lamb marinated in yogurt and spices, and grilled on skewers.

cabbage chachchari (chorchori) Bengali dish of stir-fried cabbage flavored with *panch phoron,* a characteristic Bengali spice mixture (see *Foods & Flavors Guide*).

cabbage foogath Anglo-Indian sauceless vegetable dish.

caju matar bhaji green peas with cashews.

NATIONAL FAVORITE **chaas** buttermilk. It is also enjoyed smoked. The smoked flavor is obtained by dropping some clarified butter, roasted cumin seeds and black rock salt on a live charcoal. A glass is placed over the coal, trapping the aromatic smoke that is given off. After a few minutes, buttermilk is poured into the smoky glass.

chaaval ki kheer rice pudding.

REGIONAL CLASSIC **chakli** crunchy, spiral-shaped sweet or savory treat made of rice flour and chickpea flour dough that has been extruded from a *chakli* mold (type of cookie press) through a star-shaped disk. Starting at the center, the extruded, rough-edged cylinder is coiled into a spiral about 2 inches in diameter and then fried.

REGIONAL CLASSIC **chana dal payasam** sweet made of a mixture of chickpeas, nuts, raw sugar and cardamom cooked in clarified butter. It is a treat featured during Kerala's 10-day harvest festival (Onam), the Malayali New Year (Vishu), as well as any special occasion.

chana pulao white chickpeas and rice.

chappati tortilla-like, round, unleavened bread made with whole-wheat flour and baked on an ungreased griddle.

chemeen peera Keralite dish of sautéed shrimp in a sauce flavored with curry leaves.

chemeen varattiyathu shrimp in tamarind sauce. It is a specialty of the Mopillah Muslim community of northern Kerala.

chettinad ka mirch murga dry (gravyless) pepper chicken. It is a specialty of the Nattukottai Chettiars, a community of traders, in the state of Tamil Nadu. See recipe, p. 62. REGIONAL CLASSIC

chewda (chevda) hot, spicy snack mixture containing puffed rice, lentils, nuts, spices, dried fruits and coconut. NATIONAL FAVORITE

chhenchki Bengali dish of finely chopped vegetables, usually flavored with *panch phoron,* the characteristic, aromatic Bengali spice mixture.

chhokka Bengali potato and pumpkin dish.

chicken cafreal Goan dish of fried chicken flavored with garlic, small chile peppers called *portugali* in Goa and vinegar or lime juice.

chikki hard crunchy sweet made of nuts or seeds cooked in sugar syrup, then cut into squares when cooled. NATIONAL FAVORITE

chile pakora savory, fritter-like snack of chile peppers coated in seasoned chickpea batter and deep-fried. It is a specialty of the city of Jodhpur in Rajasthan. See *bhajia,* this *Guide.* REGIONAL CLASSIC

chingri macher malai Bengali specialty dish of shrimp in a rich, red coconut-milk sauce. Also called *chingri malaikari.* See recipe, p. 59. DELICIOUS

cholar dal lightly sweetened dish of spicy lentils (typically *chana dal*), and coconut. It is a Bengali specialty.

chunda (chundo) sweet-and-sour pickle made with shredded mango. NATIONAL FAVORITE

churma caramelized, crumbly mixture of pulverized *batti* (dense whole-wheat roll) baked with powdered sugar or raw sugar and melted clarified butter. Sometimes cardamom, nuts and dried fruit are added. See *dal batti churma,* this *Guide.*

churma ladoo Gujarati version of the round sweet known as *ladoo.* It is made with whole-wheat flour, grated coconut and poppy seed. See *boondi ladoo,* this *Guide.*

chuttulli mullet boned, butterflied mullet spread with roasted spices on the flesh side and grilled. The dish typically is served with potatoes and okra stuffed with the same spice mixture used for the fish. It is a traditional dish from the once-thriving Jewish community of Fort Cochin in Kerala.

dahi mach Bengali dish of fish cooked in yogurt and spices.

NATIONAL FAVORITE **dahi vada (wada)** deep-fried balls made with a batter of ground lentils, served in creamy yogurt. There are many regional variations. In northern India *dahi vada* is topped with sweet and sour tamarind chutney.

REGIONAL CLASSIC **dal batti churma** specialty of Rajasthan consisting of three separate dishes served together as a meal. The *dal,* a mixture of one or more lentils slow-cooked in clarified butter, is eaten with *batti,* a small, dense whole-wheat roll that is pressed to crack open its crust and drizzled with clarified butter. The third meal component, *churma,* is a caramelized, crumbly mixture of pulverized *batti* baked with powdered sugar or raw sugar and melted clarified butter. Sometimes cardamom, nuts and dried fruit are added.

dal dhokri split yellow lentils flavored with a ground spice mixture containing blackened coconut, and cooked with diamond-shaped pieces of rolled, wheat-flour *chappati* dough.

dal gosht lamb and lentil curry.

TASTY **dal makhani** buttery Punjabi dish of black lentils (*urad dal*), sometimes also combined with red kidney beans. It is a dish from the northwest frontier. Also called *kali dal makhani, kali dal* and *mah ki dal*. See recipe, p. 50.

dal vada deep-fried "doughnuts" made from a paste of water-soaked ground lentils. Also simply called *vada*. It is a specialty of southern India.

dalma spicy dish of chopped vegetables cooked with split yellow lentils (*arhar dal*). It is a specialty of the state of Orissa in eastern India.

GOOD CHOICE **dhansak** one-dish meal containing chunks of lamb, vegetables and several kinds of lentils served with caramelized rice. It is a favorite dish of the Parsi community. Also called mutton *dhansak*.

REGIONAL CLASSIC **dhokla** steamed cakes made from a batter of lightly fermented rice flour and ground lentils (*urad dal*). The batter is mixed with a spice paste, steamed in a rimmed flat pan and cut into squares or diamonds when done. Some chopped cilantro and sputtered mustard seeds often are sprinkled on top. It is a snack specialty of Gujarat. Also called *khatta dhokla*. In Rajasthan, *dhokla* is made with corn.

do piyaza northern Indian curry dish made with meat, fish or seafood and lots of fried onions. Some of the onions become softened in the sauce; the rest are added toward the end of cooking so they remain crunchy.

doi begun Bengali dish of fried eggplant in yogurt and spices.

doodh pak creamy rice dessert with ground cardamom. It is a specialty of the state of Gujarat.

doodhi chana northern Indian dish of bottle gourd with lentils (*chana dal*).

dosa crispy crêpe made with soaked rice and lentils (*urad dal*) ground to a paste and fermented briefly for taste. This southern Indian specialty usually is filled with a dry vegetable mixture. Coconut chutney and *sambhar* typically accompany the crêpes. Variations of *dosa* include ones that don't have fillings or that have different ingredients in the batter. NATIONAL FAVORITE

dum arvi taro cooked in clarified butter and flavored with ginger, coriander, paprika, *garam masala* (a spice mixture) and green chile peppers. *Dum arvi* is cooked in a sealed pot, allowing it to cook in its own steam.

dum ka mutton mutton cooked in a sealed pot.

ekoori spicy Parsi dish of soft scrambled eggs with onions, tomatoes, green chile peppers and cilantro. Also spelled *akuri*.

elaichi chai cardamom tea. REFRESHING

elaichi China grass cardamom-flavored milk pudding using agar (China grass), a vegetable substitute for gelatin, to gel the mixture. See *Foods & Flavors Guide*. REGIONAL CLASSIC

elaichi gosht lamb with cardamom.

enai katrikey aromatic, sautéed eggplant. See recipe, p. 45.

era varuval Chettinad dish of fried shrimp.

erachi olarthiyathu Keralite dish of meat cooked in fresh coconut.

falooda rose-flavored milk drink containing scoops of Indian ice cream, rice- or corn-flour noodles, cubes of colored gelatin and basil seeds. This traditional Muslim drink is served in special glasses that are narrower at the base and broader at the rim. The noodles, also called *falooda,* typically garnish a dish of Indian ice cream. REGIONAL CLASSIC

faras bean bhaji Maharashtrian dish of stir-fried string beans flavored with *goda masala,* a regional spice mixture colored black by coconut that has been dry-roasted until dark.

feni aromatic liquor distilled from the juice of the cashew fruit (cashew apple) or from the juice (sap) drawn from unopened flowers of the coconut palm. It is a specialty of Goa.

firni milk pudding with rice. See *phirni,* this *Guide*. REGIONAL CLASSIC

gaboli dish of fish roe in thick curry sauce. It is a specialty of Mumbai (Bombay).

gaja fried circles of dough coated with sugar syrup. It is a specialty of Rishra, West Bengal.

NATIONAL FAVORITE **gajar halva (halwa)** sweet made with carrots, milk and nuts. It is a specialty of northern India.

gajar ka pulao rice pilaf with shredded carrots and coconut.

galawat kabab fried, melt-in-the-mouth lamb patties tenderized with papaya. See recipe, p. 41.

REGIONAL CLASSIC **gatte** chickpea flour dumplings flavored with asafoetida and other spices. Dough for *gatte* is kneaded, rolled into cylinders about ¾ inch in diameter and steamed. The cylinders are then cut into approximately 1-inch lengths and simmered in a yogurt-based curry. *Gatte* is a specialty of Jaipur, Rajasthan.

gatte ka saag Rajasthani dish of chickpea flour dumplings and spinach.

gatte ki khichiri Rajasthani dish of chickpea flour dumplings with rice and lentils.

ghar ke chaamp vinegar-flavored ribs.

ghee bhat rice fried in clarified butter.

REGIONAL CLASSIC **ghewar** round, fried dessert with a crunchy, honeycombed texture and hollow center. It is made from a batter of flour, milk, sugar, clarified butter and farmer's cheese. To obtain the dessert's characteristic shape and texture, a large spoonful of batter is poured into the center of a hot, round-bottomed pan containing some clarified butter. The batter spreads in a fine network away from the center. The height of the dessert is increased by pouring additional spoonfuls of batter in the center of the pan, which spread out over the previous layers. Sweetened milk, ground cardamom and chopped pistachio nuts typically top the dessert. It is a specialty of Jaipur, Rajasthan.

Goan fish curry classic fish curry from Goa known by its English name. The hot, sweet and sour sauce includes coconut, tomatoes and red chile peppers.

gobhi musallum cauliflower with coconut, coriander and cayenne pepper.

WONDERFUL **gobhi paratha** triangular-shaped, griddle-fried, flatbread stuffed with a grated cauliflower mixture.

gobhi tamater cauliflower with tomatoes.

YUMMY **golgappa** popular street snack using thin-walled, hollow balls made from rolled circles of bread dough that balloon up when fried in oil. The ball is stuffed with a mixture of potatoes, bean sprouts and chickpeas topped with some chutney, and then filled up with a spicy water mixture. *Golgappa* is best eaten in a single bite. Also called *pani puri*.

gosht biryani mutton or lamb marinated in spices and topped with rice, steamed in its own juices.

gosht curry popular northern Indian meat dish made with mutton or lamb stewed in a turmeric-flavored tomato and onion sauce.

gosht shahjani mutton or lamb stew with potatoes and onions, flavored with ginger, turmeric, cinnamon, cloves and cilantro.

goshtaba Kashmiri dish of meatballs made of finely pounded lamb in a thin yogurt sauce. SUPER

gucchi pulao mushroom pilaf.

Gujarati kadhi sweetened yogurt and chickpea-flour curry.

gul pohe pounded rice with raw sugar.

gulab jamun balls made of reduced milk, flour and cardamon, which are deep-fried until golden and soaked in rose-flavored sugar syrup. NATIONAL FAVORITE

gulkhand burfi rose-flavored fudge.

haleem spicy porridge-like mixture of minced lamb and cracked wheat topped with caramelized onions. This Moghlai specialty of Hyderabad is eaten during Ramadan at the end of the daily fast. REGIONAL CLASSIC

handvo Gujarati savory vegetable cake.

hari dhaniya ki chutney chutney made with cilantro.

hari roti griddle-fried flatbread made from whole-wheat flour, cooked and mashed green peas, lime juice, mint or cilantro and clarified butter.

holige griddle-cooked sweet made of small circles of dough filled with a paste of lentils and raw sugar. Also called *puran poli, puran puri* and *meetha paratha*. REGIONAL CLASSIC

idiappam steamed noodles made by extruding a batter of ground rice through a special press. It is a popular breakfast item in southern India enjoyed with sweetened coconut milk. Other names for *idiappam* are *semige* and string hoppers.

idli steamed rice and lentil (*urad dal*) "cake" traditionally enjoyed in southern India during any meal, but especially for breakfast, along with *sambhar,* a dish of lentils and vegetables, and coconut chutney. NATIONAL FAVORITE

imli ki chutney tamarind chutney.

GREAT **jalebi (jelebi)** deep-fried sweet soaked in saffron-flavored sugar syrup. A batter of flour and yogurt is piped in pencil-thin strands onto the surface of hot oil in a pattern of loops resembling a row of several pretzels linked together.

REGIONAL CLASSIC **jaljeera** cumin-flavored, sweet-and-sour cooler with ginger, tamarind, raw sugar and other spices. It also is drunk as a digestive. Another name for this drink is *jeera pani.*

jardaloo ma gosht lamb stew with dried apricots; it is a specialty of the Parsi community.

jeera pani cumin-flavored drink; see *jaljeera.*

jeera pulao cumin-flavored rice.

jhinga ka pulao rice with shrimp.

REGIONAL CLASSIC **jhol** Bengali thin curry.

kabuli chana curried chickpeas.

kachhe gosht ki biryani classic and elaborate Moghlai dish of lamb and rice. See recipe, p. 53.

kachi kaliya gravied Moghlai dish of goat and potatoes. It is a specialty of Kolkata (Calcutta).

kaddu ki subji pumpkin cooked in spices.

REGIONAL CLASSIC **kadhi** chickpea dumplings in yogurt sauce. It is a dish from northern Punjab.

kaiadai deep-fried dessert made with balls of banana paste stuffed with a sweetened mixture of dried fruits and nuts. It is a treat of the Mopillah Muslim community of northern Kerala, and is made with a banana called *nendra kai* grown in the southern part of Kerala.

kair dakh Rajasthani dish of raisins and wild, berry-like fruits in a yogurt-based sauce flavored with turmeric, coriander, cumin, garlic and cayenne pepper.

kair sangri kumita dish made with three desert famine foods: a small, berry-like fruit (*kair*) grown on a leafless, thorny tree in arid regions of the state of Rajasthan, along with a small bean pod (*sangri*) that grows on a different thorny tree and another desert berry called *kumita*. These foods are available when all other vegetation in the Thar desert has dried up. This dish is identified with one of the Rajasthani communities, the Marwari, based around Jodhpur.

kairi ki laungi green mangoes in a spicy sauce rich in cloves.

kaju chi poli soft pancake filled with sweetened ground cashews, eaten as a dessert.

kaju ki subji stir-fried cashews.

kakori kabab kebab of minced lamb tenderized with papaya and given a smoky flavor by putting the mince in a bowl surrounding a glowing coal topped with clarified butter. To make the kebab, a ball of meat is put on a special 3-foot long skewer with a 3/8-inch diameter, and massaged into a sausage shape. Traditionally, it is cooked in a *tandoori* oven. The dish is attributed to the Moghals of Awadh (Lucknow today). It is named after Kakori, a small town near Lucknow in Uttar Pradesh. Also called *seekh kabab*. **WONDERFUL**

kalan Keralite dish of bananas in a yogurt and coconut sauce flavored with green chile peppers and black mustard seeds.

kalan thoren mushroom stir-fry.

kali dal makhani creamy black lentils (*urad dal*). See *dal makhani*. Also called *mah ki dal* and simply *kali dal*.

kallum makkai stuffed mussels (stone fruit). Mussels are opened, stuffed with a paste of ground rice and grated coconut flavored with anise and cumin, and steamed. The contents are then removed from the shell, briefly marinated in a light sauce of turmeric and chile pepper, and fried. It is a specialty of Tellicherry, Kerala. **REGIONAL CLASSIC**

kandarpam deep-fried balls made of a flour and raw sugar mixture. It is a specialty of Chennai, Tamil Nadu.

kandyachi bhaji onion fritters.

kankrar jhal Bengali dish of crab in hot pepper curry sauce.

kannan pathiri type of fried bread made of wheat and rice flour. Small balls of dough are rolled out and folded into a square shape, then turned over and folded to make flaps resembling an envelope. When the bread is fried, it puffs up and the pattern of the folds is said to resemble an eye (*kannan*). It is a specialty of the Mopillah Muslim community of northern Kerala. **REGIONAL CLASSIC**

karanji crescent-shaped pastries filled with a mixture of coconut flavored with saffron and cardamom. It is a treat enjoyed during Diwali, a Hindu holiday; see *Foods & Flavors Guide*. Also see *modak*.

karimeen pollichathu fillets of silver fish (or whole small silver fish) marinated in a vinegary spice mixture and cooked in banana leaves. It is a regional specialty of Kerala. **REGIONAL CLASSIC**

karimeen porichathu silver fish sautéed in oil and spices. It is a regional specialty of Kerala.

katachi amti Maharashtrian curry with chickpeas, typically served with rice.

kathi kabab chunks of marinated meat grilled and wrapped in a *paratha,* a griddle-fried flatbread. It is fast food originating in Kolkata (Calcutta). Also called *kathi roll.*

kedgeree classic dish of lentils, rice and spices—known to Indians as *khichri*—that the British colonials altered by adding fish or meat, calling it *kedgeree.*

kela kofte savory balls made of mashed green bananas.

kesar bhat sweet saffron rice flavored with cardamom.

NATIONAL FAVORITE **kesari sooji halwa** bright-yellow, saffron-flavored halva made with semolina, clarified butter and sugar. Also called *sooji halwa.*

kewra sherbet cooler flavored with screwpine essence.

khakhra crispy, thin, Gujarati-style bread made from whole-wheat and white flours and flavored with *garam masala.* It is roasted on a hot griddle. A pale green version has finely chopped fenugreek leaves.

khamang kakadi spicy grated cucumber salad.

REGIONAL CLASSIC **khandvi** Gujarati dish of rolled strips, about two-inches wide, cut from chickpea flour "pancakes." The rolls are topped with chopped cilantro, grated coconut and a sautéed mixture of curry leaves, asafoetida and chopped green chile peppers.

khasta roti unleavened whole-wheat bread often flavored with *ajwain* seeds.

khatta dhokla steamed cakes made with a lightly fermented batter of rice flour and ground lentils (*urad dal*). See *dhokla.*

khatta moong sour (tart) mung beans.

khatti machi baked fish in a sour (tart) sauce.

YUMMY **khatti mithi gohbi** sweet and sour cauliflower.

kheema karela mixture of minced bitter gourd and meat.

kheema mater minced lamb with green peas. It is a Punjabi favorite.

NATIONAL FAVORITE **kheer** milk pudding, often containing rice.

REGIONAL CLASSIC **kheera raita** yogurt with cucumber, typically flavored with cumin and cayenne pepper. See recipe, p. 49.

kheera tamater ka raita cucumber and tomato in yogurt.

khichri dish of lentils, rice and spices. The British colonials altered the dish by adding fish and called it *kedgeree.*

khubani ka mitha Hyderabadi dish of stewed, dried apricots sprinkled with almonds and topped with cream.

khus-khus ki chutney poppy seed chutney.

kiskiya whole-wheat porridge cooked with minced meat and spices. It is a favorite dish of southern Indian Muslims.

kizhangu curried potatoes cooked in a mixture of spices and roasted coconut.

kobi zunka Maharashtrian dish of cabbage with a crumbled paste of cooked chickpea flour and spices.

kokum kadi slightly tart drink of fresh coconut milk flavored and colored pink with the dried rind of the red mango fruit. Also called *sol kadi*. TASTY

Kolhapuri rassa lamb in a spicy, coconut curry sauce. It is a specialty of Kolhapur, a city in Maharashtra.

komdi vindaloo spicy Goan chicken curry. REGIONAL CLASSIC

kootu southern Indian dish of lentils with vegetables and coconut.

kozhi mulug varathathu Keralite preparation of chicken cooked in coconut oil with green chile peppers and spices.

kulfa bhaje Hyderabadi dish of spinach and chickpeas.

kulfi Indian ice cream. It typically is served with rice or corn noodles flavored with screwpine essence. DELICIOUS

kulith saar soup made with horse gram (a type of lentil).

kulith usal stir-fried horse gram (a type of lentil).

kurmura laddoo sweet balls made with puffed rice.

kuthari choru Keralite dish of parboiled, unpolished red rice.

kuttige rice and lentil (*urad dal*) batter steamed in jackfruit leaves. It is a popular breakfast dish in Mangalore.

kuzhambu reduced tamarind sauce used with plain rice or rice with yogurt.

ladoo ball-shaped sweet. A common one, *boondi ladoo,* is made from deep-fried chickpea flour droplets (*boondi*) and other ingredients such as nuts and raisins. It is eaten at special events and parties, but is unlikely to be found on menus. NATIONAL FAVORITE

lahsun chutney hot garlic chutney.

lahsun paratha garlic-flavored flatbread made of whole-wheat flour and clarified butter.

lal maans (maas) red lamb stew. It is the favorite lamb dish of Rajasthan, and its spicy yogurt gravy is rich in red chile peppers. Also called *lamb korma*. See recipe, p. 50. GOOD CHOICE

lassi yogurt-based drink that can be sweet or salty and have any number of flavor variations. NATIONAL FAVORITE

lau ghanto Bengali dish of chopped bottle gourd with coconut and green peas.

YUMMY **lauki ka halwa** sweet made with grated, cooked bottle gourd, reduced milk, sugar and clarified butter. Often chopped almonds and blond raisins are added. Also called *lauki pak.*

Ledikeni Bengali sweet created in the 19th century to celebrate the birthday of Lady Canning, wife of the first Viceroy of India. To make it, balls of farmer's cheese mixed with semolina are filled with thickened, reduced milk flavored with cardamom. The balls are fried in clarified butter until golden and soaked in sugar syrup.

lobhia ki subzi spicy black-eyed peas.

lukmi deep-fried squares of dough made of all-purpose flour and clarified butter filled with a savory minced lamb mixture. It is a specialty of Hyderabad.

REGIONAL CLASSIC **macchi Amritsari** Punjabi dish of fish dredged in a mixture of chickpea flour, garlic and onion paste, paprika and *ajwain* seeds. The town of Amritsar in Punjab is home to the Golden Temple, which is sacred to those of the Sikh faith.

REGIONAL CLASSIC **machher jhol** Bengali dish of fish marinated in mustard seed paste, then lightly fried and stewed in a spicy curry sauce.

machi no sas Parsi dish of fish with eggs.

maghaj cardamom-flavored sweet made from chickpea flour, clarified butter and thickened, reduced milk.

mah ki dal creamy black lentils (*urad dal*). See *dal makhani.* Also called *kali dal* and *kali dal makhani.*

REGIONAL CLASSIC **makkhan malai** preparation of frothy cream flavored with saffron and screwpine, and topped with silver leaf. To make the dish, boiled milk is put on the rooftop overnight, covered with a cloth. Dew settles on the cream that has risen to the top of milk, and this layer is removed and whipped. *Makkhan malai* is a breakfast specialty of Lucknow, the capital of the state of Uttar Pradesh.

Malabar jhinga kadhi shrimp curry made slightly sour with the dried rind of the red mango. The Malabar Coast is a narrow strip of fertile, rice-growing land stretching from Goa to the southern tip of India (Cape Comorin).

REGIONAL CLASSIC **malai kofta** fried balls of farmer's cheese cooked in a creamy, tomato-based gravy.

malai mater peas in cream.

malaikari Bengali sauce of coconut milk and clarified butter flavored with a special mixture of spices called *garam masala.*

malpua round, sugar-soaked sweet made from a batter of flour, semolina and milk. It has a spongy center, crisp edges and is topped with a sweet fennel syrup drizzled with cream. Also called *malpuri.* REGIONAL CLASSIC

masala chai spicy tea made with milk, sugar, cardamom, cloves, cinnamon, ginger and black pepper. See recipe, p. 66. NATIONAL FAVORITE

masala dal spicy yellow lentils.

masala dosa crispy crêpe made from a batter of ground rice and lentils (*urad dal*) and folded over a potato stuffing. It is a specialty of southern India. NATIONAL FAVORITE

masale bhat spicy rice pilaf.

masoor dal popular, everyday dish of spicy red lentils.

matar gohbi peas and cauliflower.

matar paneer peas with farmer's cheese. REGIONAL CLASSIC

matar pulao rice pilaf with peas.

matki ambat moth bean and coconut curry.

matki usal (ussul) sprouted moth beans stir-fried with spices and grated coconut.

meen moiley fish in a creamy coconut sauce. It is a classic dish from the southern state of Kerala. See recipe, p. 60. REGIONAL CLASSIC

meen pattichathu Keralite dish of dried fish cooked in a sauce that is flavored and soured with the dried rind of the red mango.

melagu vegetables cooked in a spice mixture with black pepper. It is a specialty of Chettinad cuisine in southern India.

methi bhajiya fritter made with chickpea flour batter with fenugreek leaves.

methi saag fresh fenugreek leaves cooked with spices. REGIONAL CLASSIC

mezhu kkuvaratti Keralite dish of beetroot sautéed in coconut oil with hot green chiles and spices.

mihidana Bengali sweet made from a paste of chickpea and wheat flours. The paste is pressed through the holes of a grater to make droplets, which are fried in clarified butter and then soaked in sugar syrup. It is a specialty of the city of Burdwan.

milakai podi ground lentils, spices and oil eaten with pieces of *idli,* steamed, fermented rice-and-lentil dumplings, or *dosa,* crispy crêpes made with ground, soaked rice and lentils. *Milakai podi* is a specialty of the southern state of Tamil Nadu.

milk burfi creamy fudge made with reduced milk, decorated with edible silver foil.

mirchi bhajia fritter-like snack of chile peppers coated in seasoned chickpea batter and deep fried. Also called *chile pakora.* REGIONAL CLASSIC

mirchi ka salan curried green chile peppers. It is a fiery specialty of Hyderabad, the capital of the state of Andhra Pradesh. The food of Andhra Pradesh is the hottest in India.

mirchi vada sweet banana peppers stuffed with a potato mixture and deep-fried in batter made of chickpea flour. It is a snack specialty of Rajasthan.

mishri mawa dessert made with sweetened milk boiled down until the liquid is gone. It is a specialty of Jaipur, in the state of Rajasthan.

REGIONAL CLASSIC **mishti doi** sweet Bengali dessert made by adding yogurt and sugar to fresh milk that has been partially condensed by boiling. The mixture sets when cooled. It traditionally is prepared in clay bowls.

GOOD CHOICE **mitha paratha** griddle-cooked sweet made of small circles of dough filled with a paste of lentils and raw sugar. Also called *holige, puran poli* and *puran puri.*

mithi chutney sweet tamarind chutney.

modak sweet, fig-shaped version of a pastry called *karanji*. It is made by putting a spoonful of sweet filling in the center of a rolled circle of dough, and folding up its edges to create a fluted, inverted cone. Because *modak* is a great favorite of Ganesh (the elephant-headed Hindu god), an honorary *modak* is first offered to him whenever *karanjis* are made. Then the rest of the dough is used to make crescent shaped pastries for mortals. See *karanji.*

moode batter of ground rice and lentils (*urad dal*) steamed in banana leaves and served with several different chutneys.

mooli dal subzi dish of radish and lentils.

REGIONAL CLASSIC **mooli paratha** griddle-fried, flatbread made from whole-wheat flour and clarified butter, which has a radish filling. It is a popular breakfast item in Uttar Pradesh.

moong ussul (usal) sprouted mung beans stir-fried with spices and grated coconut. See recipe, p. 49.

moori breakfast dish of puffed rice with fruit.

moti pulao saffron-flavored rice pilaf garnished with small, deep-fried balls made of farmer's cheese, finely ground cashews and cornflour, and covered with a paper-thin sheet of edible silver foil. The dish is a specialty of Lucknow, Uttar Pradesh.

motipak sweet made of deep-fried droplets of chickpea flour batter and held together with sugar syrup. The mixture is formed into small balls, placed in paper cups and topped with dried fruits, nuts and pieces of edible silver foil.

mulligatawny curried soup with chunks of meat in a meat stock flavored with onion, garlic, chile pepper, coriander, cumin and fenugreek. Many variations exist. The name of the soup is a corruption of the Tamil (a southern Indian language) words *milagu* and *tunni* meaning "pepper water." With the advent of the British Raj (British rule in India) in the mid 18th century, the name took on the meaning of a soup and the colonial British ate it as a separate course. This contrasted with Indian meals, which were not served in courses, and anything resembling a soup was a thin sauce eaten along with everything else in the meal.

murgh biryani spicy chicken with rice.

murgh dhansak classic Parsi dish of chicken with lentils.

murgh hariyali chicken in green *masala* (spice paste), typically a mixture of ground mint leaves, cilantro and hot green chile peppers.

murgh jhal frezie a hot dish from British India containing chicken, vegetables, onion, chile peppers and spices. EXCELLENT

murgh ka mokul Rajasthani dish of shredded chicken in yogurt and cashew sauce flavored with saffron and ginger. The dish traditionally was made with shredded rabbit. See recipe, p. 56.

murgh pakora marinated pieces of chicken breast coated in batter made with chickpea flour and deep-fried.

murgh rashida chicken garnished with eggs.

murgh roghni Moghlai dish of chicken in almond and cashew sauce.

murgh tikka butter masala barbecued chicken in buttery tomato and cream sauce. See recipe, p. 57. NATIONAL FAVORITE

muri ghonto Bengali dish of curried fish head soup. Carp (either *katla* or *rohu*) is the preferred type of fish used to make *muri ghonto.*

mutton dhansak one-dish meal containing chunks of lamb, vegetables and several kinds of lentils served with caramelized rice. It is a favorite dish of the Parsi community. Also simply called *dhansak.* REGIONAL CLASSIC

mutton kola minced meatballs cooked in a curry sauce.

mutton kolhapuri dish of spicy lamb named for the town of Kolhapur, near Mumbai (Bombay), which is famous for its dried, hot red chile peppers. See recipe, p. 61. REGIONAL CLASSIC

mutton nally mutton stew using bone-in pieces of meat.

mutton talai kari dish of mutton head in curry sauce.

mysore pak southern Indian sweet made from chickpea flour mixed with clarified butter cooked in boiling sugar syrup. After the mixture cools and sets, it is cut into small squares. REGIONAL CLASSIC

NATIONAL FAVORITE **naan** flat, leavened white bread traditionally cooked in a *tandoori* oven. See recipe, p. 63.

nadru pakora Kashmiri deep-fried pieces of lotus stem pounded flat and coated in spicy chickpea flour batter.

REGIONAL CLASSIC **nargisi kofta** hard-boiled egg covered with a spicy minced meat mixture and deep-fried. It is served with gravy.

nariyal palak spinach with coconut. See recipe, p. 44.

REGIONAL CLASSIC **navratan korma** mixture of vegetables, dried fruits and nuts in a thick gravy.

neer dosai griddle-fried crêpe made with unfermented batter made of ground raw rice and coconut.

neer more southern Indian buttermilk drink.

REGIONAL CLASSIC **nimbu chaval** lemon rice. See recipe, p. 42.

nimbu pani sweet or salty lime drink. The sweet version is also called *shikanji.*

nimbu sherbet lemon drink flavored with ground, roasted cumin seeds.

noodle upma southern Indian breakfast dish of noodles cooked in spicy broth.

omanapura crêpe made from ground rice and a type of lentil (*urad dal*), which is topped with a shredded meat mixture and rolled up like a jellyroll. Two sides of the circle are folded to the center before rolling to help keep the contents from spilling out. The roll is then fried in a little vegetable oil. It is a traditional starter dish in the Mopillah Muslim community of northern Kerala. Also called *alisi.*

REGIONAL CLASSIC **oondhiyoon** Gujarati dish of mixed vegetables.

osaman Gujarati dish of lentils cooked in tamarind water.

pach koota traditional famine food preparation of the Marwari community in western Rajasthani. The mixture contains five desert foods: four desert bean pods and fruits (*kair, sangri, kumita* and *babool*), and one resin (*goondi*), along with garlic, oil and whole red chile peppers for color. It is boiled with dried mango to soften the ingredients and to sour the mixture. Traditionally *pach koota* was packed by travelers as road food because it kept well. The desert pods and fruits are eaten not only during times of famine, and they exported for consumption by the Indian diaspora.

pachadi Keralite dish of chopped cucumber in yogurt-based sauce with mustard and coconut.

pakora savory, fritter-like snack of sliced vegetables, especially onion rings, coated in seasoned chickpea batter and deep-fried. It once was important food for travelers. Another name for *pakora* is *bhajia (bhajiya)*. Snacks are also made of fried batter without the addition of vegetables, and these are called *bondas*. NATIONAL FAVORITE

palak paneer spinach with farmer's cheese. See recipe, p. 46. YUMMY

paneer makhni pieces of farmer's cheese cooked in a spicy, tomato-based mixture with cream.

paneer naan *tandoori*-baked flatbread stuffed with farmer's cheese.

pani puri popular street snack using thin-walled, hollow balls made from rolled circles of bread dough that balloon up when fried in oil. The ball is stuffed with a mixture of potatoes, bean sprouts and chickpeas topped with some chutney, and then filled up with a spicy water mixture. *Pani puri* is best eaten in a single bite. Also called *golgappa*. NATIONAL FAVORITE

paniarum small balls made of lentil flour batter, which are fried in a special skillet with depressions that hold the batter.

panki chatni savory rice pancakes cooked between banana leaves and served with yogurt.

pantua balls of farmer's cheese fried in clarified butter and soaked in sugar syrup. It is a specialty of West Bengal.

papad ki subji thin, round wafers (*pappadams*) made of lentils and spices served in a spicy gravy.

paper dosa large (about 2 feet in diameter) crêpe made from a batter of ground rice and lentils (*urad dal*). NATIONAL FAVORITE

paper masala dosa large (about 2 feet in diameter) crêpe made from a batter of ground rice and lentils (*urad dal*), which is folded over a spicy potato mixture.

parra fish pickled in vinegar and spices.

patol dolma Bengali dish of stuffed, pointed gourd. Meat or flaked fish are common stuffings.

patra ni machi Parsi dish of fish coated with green chutney, wrapped in banana leaves and steamed.

paturi mach Bengali fish dish made with *illisher,* a popular fish found in the estuaries of the Bay of Bengal. The fish, called *hilsa* in Hindi, is marinated in mustard oil and spices, wrapped in banana leaves and steamed. The mustardy, oily sauce produced in the cooking process is served with rice. Also called *bhalolaga illisher paturi*. See recipe, p. 58. REGIONAL CLASSIC

pavta batata Maharastrian dish of potato with lima beans.

payasam southern Indian milk-based dessert with rice or vermicelli, sugar and cashews. A darker version has palm sugar.

payeesh rice pudding made with milk and palm sugar.

REGIONAL CLASSIC **phirni** disk-shaped sweet composed of fine threads of dough. To form it, small balls of dough made of all-purpose flour, milk and clarified butter are pulled into an "o" shape, folded back into a smaller "o" and then twisted into a figure eight, repeatedly, until the dough breaks up into threads. It is a specialty of Jaipur in the state of Rajasthan. Also the name for a blancmange-like dish made with rice, pistachios and almonds, flavored with screwpine extract. Another spelling is *firni*.

phool ghobi bhajia cauliflower fritter.

pinaca Goan sweet made of a mixture of roasted rice, palm sugar, grated coconut and water.

pista burfi milk-based fudge with pistachios.

pista dal kachori small, deep-fried breads filled with a savory paste of ground lentils and pistachios.

REGIONAL CLASSIC **pittore** spicy chickpea flour "dumplings" in a yogurt-based sauce. See recipe, p. 51.

piyaz ki chutney onion chutney.

REGIONAL CLASSIC **podi uthapam (uddapam)** type of thicker *dosa* (crêpe made with soaked rice and lentils ground to a paste and fermented briefly for taste) with minced vegetables in the batter. It is a specialty of the states of Tamil Nadu and Karnatka.

pongal sweet rice porridge. Also the name of a savory rice and lentil dish.

poothotta konju Keralite dish of shrimp curry with fermented palm juice (toddy) flavored with dried rind of the red mango.

GREAT CHOICE **pork vindaloo** classic Goan hot and sour pork curry with vinegar.

pudina dosa crispy crêpe made with soaked rice and lentils (*urad dal*) ground to a paste, with bits of chopped mint in the batter.

pudina ka sherbet refreshing drink make with fresh mint and flavored with ginger.

NATIONAL FAVORITE **pudina ki chutney** mint chutney.

pulao rice pilaf.

puli shaadam tamarind rice.

puneri dal dish of yellow lentils with *goda masala,* a spice mixture containing grated coconut that has been dry roasted until dark, palm sugar and curry leaves. The dish and the spice mixture is a specialty of Pune, a city in the state of Maharashtra.

punjabi chole spicy chickpea curry. It is a specialty of northern India. NATIONAL FAVORITE

puran poli griddle-cooked sweet made of small circles of dough filled with a paste of lentils and raw sugar. Also called *holige, puran puri* and *meetha paratha.* REGIONAL CLASSIC

puri deep-fried bread made from whole-wheat flour and clarified butter.

puri bhaji deep-fried bread made from whole-wheat flour and clarified butter served with sauceless vegetables stir-fried with spices and a little oil. NATIONAL FAVORITE

raan mussallam baked leg of lamb marinated in a yogurt spice mixture and basted in clarified butter.

rabori pieces of corn *papadam* (thin, round wafer usually made of lentils) in a yogurt and chile pepper sauce.

rabri northern Indian milk-based dessert garnished with nuts and cardamom. During the process of reducing the milk by cooking, the skin that forms on the surface of the milk is swept continuously to the side of the pan. These pieces give the dish texture. DELICIOUS

rajma Punjabi dish of spicy red kidney beans cooked in a tomato-based sauce. REGIONAL CLASSIC

rajma ka salad red kidney bean salad.

rasam spicy southern Indian broth made from cooked, mashed lentils (*toorvar dal*) and tomatoes. It is eaten with rice or drunk as a beverage. REGIONAL CLASSIC

ratan pulao mixed vegetable pilaf.

rava dosa thin crêpe made of rice flour and semolina with chopped green chile peppers, cumin seeds and mustard seeds.

rava idli small steamed cake made from semolina and rice flour batter.

rava ladoo sweet made of semolina toasted in clarified butter, grated coconut, sugar, cardamom, almonds and raisins, mixed together with sugar syrup and formed into small balls.

rava upma (uppuma) mixture of cooked semolina, chile peppers and spices. It is a popular breakfast dish in southern India.

rista Kashmiri dish of meatballs made of finely pounded lamb cooked in a saffron-flavored sauce with red chile peppers, and colored red with an extract of cockscomb flowers. WONDERFUL

rogan (roghan) josh traditional hot Kashmiri dish of lamb in a yogurt sauce flavored with cinnamon, cardamom, cloves, cayenne REGIONAL CLASSIC pepper, paprika, ginger and fennel. Also called *rogan gosht.* A similar dish called *passanda,* which is made with beef, is more apt to be found in Pakistan, because Hindus abstain from eating beef for religious reasons.

rogani (rogni) roti round, flatbread made of whole-wheat flour, milk and clarified butter, which is cooked very slowly on a griddle without oil. The bread is pressed while cooking to let the butter escape and give the surface an even color.

NATIONAL FAVORITE **rossogolla** Bengali sweet made of balls of farmer's cheese cooked in sugar syrup.

roti griddle-cooked, round, flatbread made of whole-wheat flour.

NATIONAL FAVORITE **saag aloo** curried spinach with potatoes.

saag gosht northern Indian dish of lamb cooked with tomato, yogurt, onion, green chile pepper, garlic, ginger, cardamom, cinnamon, ginger, turmeric, chile powder and spinach.

sabudana khichri savory mixture of sago pearls, diced potatoes, green chile pepper, ginger, cumin and finely ground peanuts. It is a specialty of the state of Maharashtra.

sabut piyaz ki dal whole onions with lentils.

sai bhaji dish of spinach with lentils, vegetables and green chile peppers. It is a breakfast specialty of the Sindhi community in western India.

sali murghi Parsi dish of spicy chicken curry with fried potato sticks.

sambaram buttermilk flavored with an extract of grated ginger, green chile peppers, shallots, cumin and curry leaves, and garnished with lime. See recipe, p. 66.

REGIONAL CLASSIC **sambhar** southern Indian dish of lentils with vegetables; it can accompany rice, fermented rice and lentil crêpes or steamed, fermented rice and lentil dumplings.

YUMMY **samosa** triangular, filled pastry. Half-circles of rolled dough are formed into a cone and stuffed, often with a potato mixture. The edges of the dough are pinched together and sealed. At the base of the cone, the edges are pinched to resemble a coil. The pastry is then fried. In West Bengal the pastry is called *shingara.*

sandesh Bengali sweet made with farmer's cheese cooked with sugar and rosewater. The mixture is then spread in a pan, decorated with nuts or raisins and cut into squares.

sangri curry *sangri* (type of desert bean pod) with gravy made with freshly made buttermilk. It is a specialty of Rajasthan.

sannas small steamed "cake" made from a batter of ground rice and lentils (*urad dal*) that is fermented with fresh toddy (palm juice). The cakes have to be made before the batter goes flat, or they won't be airy. This Goan specialty is eaten with *sorpotel,* a spicy and vinegary dish of pork and liver.

sarangya che bhujane pomfret slices cooked in a mixture of onions, ginger-garlic paste, cilantro and spices. It is a specialty of the Pathare Prabhu community of the city of Mumbai (Bombay) in the state of Maharashtra. REGIONAL CLASSIC

sarson ka saag dish of mustard greens sautéed in clarified butter with onion and tomato. It is a winter specialty of Punjab. GREAT

saunf ki chai fennel tea.

seekh kabab kebab of minced lamb tenderized with papaya and given a smoky flavor by putting the mince in a bowl surrounding a coal topped with clarified butter. To make the kebab, a ball of meat is put on a special 3-foot long skewer with a wider than usual diameter (3/8-inch), and massaged into a sausage shape. It traditionally is cooked in a *tandoori* oven. The dish is attributed to the Moghals of Awadh (Lucknow today). Also called *kakori kabab,* named after a small town near Lucknow in Uttar Pradesh. NATIONAL FAVORITE

semige steamed noodles made by extruding a batter of ground rice through a special press. It is a popular breakfast item in southern India enjoyed with sweetened coconut milk. Other names for *semige* are *idiappam* and string hoppers.

sevian kheer milk pudding with toasted Indian vermicelli, nuts and dates or raisins. Also called *sheer khurma*. See recipe, p. 65. NATIONAL FAVORITE

shab deg curried lamb meatballs and turnip roundels flavored with saffron. The meat and vegetable balls are purposely made the same size to look identical. The dish is attributed to the Moghals of Awadh (Lucknow today).

shahi korma spicy lamb with almonds and cream.

shakuti Goan dish of chicken or lamb in coconut gravy.

shami kabab patty made with minced lamb containing lentils (*chana dal*) and spices, and stuffed with a mixture of onion, chile peppers, ginger, cilantro and green (unripe) mango. The dish is attributed to the Moghals of Awadh (Lucknow today).

sheer khurma milk pudding with toasted Indian vermicelli, nuts and dates or raisins. Also called *sevian kheer*. See recipe, p. 65.

sheermal sweet, round, leavened, flatbread made from all-purpose flour, eggs, milk, sugar and clarified butter. After it is baked—traditionally in a *tandoori* oven—it is basted in a saffron-milk solution. REGIONAL CLASSIC

shikampur Hyderabadi dish of seasoned minced lamb patties stuffed with an onion and yogurt mixture.

shikanji sweet lime drink. Also called *nimbu pani.*

shingara triangular, filled pastry. Half-circles of rolled dough are formed into a cone and stuffed, often with a potato mixture. The edges of the dough are pinched together and sealed. At the base of the cone, the edges are pinched to resemble a coil. The pastry is then fried. In West Bengal the pastry is called *samosa.*

REGIONAL CLASSIC **shrikhand** western Indian sweet dessert made of strained yogurt, flavored with saffron and cardamom and garnished with pistachios or *chirongi,* the lentil-sized brown fruit kernels from a tree of the cashew family.

shukto curried bitter gourd.

simla mirchi bhajiya stuffed bell pepper coated in seasoned chickpea flour batter and fried.

sita bhog Bengali sweet made of cardamom-flavored threads of dough. To make it, a mixture of farmer's cheese, all-purpose flour, rice flour, sugar and clarified butter is extruded through a special press. The threads are fried until golden and soaked in hot sugar-syrup, or extruded directly into the hot sugar-syrup.

REGIONAL CLASSIC **sohan papadi** Rajasthani sweet made with milk reduced by cooking until thick and clarified butter, flavored with cardamom or rose water.

sol kadhi cold coconut-milk drink flavored with dried rind of the red mango. Also called *kokum kadi.*

sooji halwa bright-yellow, saffron-flavored halva made with semolina, clarified butter and sugar. Also called *kesari sooji halwa.*

sorpotel spicy and vinegary dish of pork and liver. *Sorpotel* is of Portuguese origin.

soweta (soyata) Rajasthani dish of millet with spices and meat. The dish is called *kheech* if meat is not added.

string hoppers see *idiappam.*

NATIONAL FAVORITE **subji ka pulao** vegetable pilaf.

suiyam sweet, deep-fried balls made of lentils (*chana dal*), coconut and palm sugar. It is a specialty of the state of Tamil Nadu.

REGIONAL CLASSIC **sukhi urad dal** gravyless lentils.

sula ka maas meat on skewers. The type of meat used depends on the region. In Rajasthan, for example, it would be lamb. If the meat is minced, the dish is called *seekh kabab.*

tali bombil marinated Bombay duck coated in spices, dipped in batter and fried.

tali kaleja fried liver.

tamater che saar tomato and coconut milk curry with spices and palm sugar. It is a specialty of southern India.

tamater pulao rice pilaf with tomatoes.

tandoori murgh Punjabi dish of red baked chicken. The meat is marinated in yogurt, cayenne pepper, powdered coriander and cumin seeds, ginger, garlic and red food coloring, and traditionally baked in a *tandoori* oven. **NATIONAL FAVORITE**

tayyar shaadum mixture of rice and yogurt enjoyed in the state of Tamil Nadu at the end of a meal to settle the stomach.

thandai cold, milk-based drink with pulverized almonds and flavored with saffron. **REGIONAL CLASSIC**

thenga chor rice cooked in coconut milk with mussels, a specialty of the Mopillah Muslim community in northern Kerala.

tulsi ka sherbet cold beverage flavored with small-leaf Indian basil.

tulsi kadha basil tea made with small-leaf Indian basil.

uddapam (uthapam) savory soft pancake of varying sizes made of fermented rice flour batter. Pancakes can be plain or topped with ingredients such as onions and hot chiles, and mixed vegetables. **REGIONAL CLASSIC**

uppuma dry, fluffy, southern Indian breakfast dish of semolina, lentils (*urad dal* and *chana dal*), bits of green and red chile peppers and spices. **REGIONAL CLASSIC**

ussul savory dish made with sprouted beans. See recipe for *moong ussul,* p. 49.

vada deep-fried "doughnuts" made of water-soaked ground lentils. This specialty of southern india is also called *dal vada.* **NATIONAL FAVORITE**

vada pan ball of spicy potato mixture covered with seasoned chickpea batter and fried. It is a popular street food in Mumbai (Bombay).

valache birde stir-fry of lentils (*val dal*) and coconut.

vangi ani val Maharashtrian dish of eggplant and lentils (*val dal*) with coconut.

varan Maharashtrian mild lentil curry made with yellow lentils (*toorvar dal*), turmeric, sugar and asafoetida.

vatana aamti Konkon curry dish of black chickpeas sautéed with onion, spices and coconut.

REGIONAL CLASSIC **vatti pathiri** round, very thin white "bread" rolled from dough made of rice flour and coconut milk, which is griddle-cooked. *Vatti pathiri* is cut with a cutter so it remains round. It is the common bread variety in restaurants in Tellicherry in northern Kerala.

REGIONAL CLASSIC **vindaloo** classic hot and sour curry with vinegar. This dish often has been billed incorrectly as the hottest of Indian dishes. The name *vindaloo* actually refers to a cooking style, not a measure of the chile pepper content of the dish. It is a specialty of Goa and is of Portuguese origin. See *pork vindaloo,* this *Guide.*

REGIONAL CLASSIC **yakhni pulao** Moghlai dish of mutton or chicken with rice that has been cooked in the broth the meat cooked in rather than in water. It is a specialty of Kashmir.

zaffran pulao saffron pilaf garnished with pieces of edible silver foil.

Foods & Flavors Guide

This chapter contains a comprehensive list of foods, spices, kitchen utensils and cooking terminology in transliterated Hindi, with English translations. About fifty percent of the population speak Hindi as their primary language.

It would be unwieldy to list each entry in several different Indian languages. We did, however, provide the local names of certain items that are associated with the cuisine in non-Hindi-speaking states. Such languages include Bengali, spoken by almost all of the population in West Bengal and much of neighboring state of Assam; Tamil, spoken in the southern state of Tamil Nadu; Malayalam, the principal language of the southern state of Kerala; and Farsi, spoken by the Parsis, the majority of whom live in the state of Maharastra.

Perhaps it will appear strange at first to see that some of the entries are in English or include English words in their name. This is the result of over 300 years of British rule; India gained independence in 1947. English is widely understood in urban centers, and is used for many official purposes.

The *Foods & Flavors Guide* will be helpful in interpreting menus and for shopping in the lively and fascinating outdoor markets. You will find that prices are indicated on food for sale in the markets but often the items themselves are not identified. Therefore, if you don't recognize something, why not inquire, "What is this called?" (see *Helpful Phrases,* p. 75). Write down the answer phonetically, and use this *Guide* to help identify it. Remember that many transliterated spellings are possible for most words.

Some ingredients used in Indian cookery may be new to you. We hope you have a chance to experience several of them. An example is *hing,* or asafoetida, a strong, sulfur-smelling, milky gum resin from the mature roots of a member of the giant fennel family (*Ferula foetida*), which is grown in Kashmir. Small amounts of powdered resin are used to enhance the flavor of dishes. In Rajasthan, try chickpea flour dumplings (*gatte*) flavored with *hing* and other spices. Another flavor that may be new to you is *kalpasi,* a lichen used as an herb.

aam mango.

aamchoor (aamchur) dried, powdered, unripe (green) mango used to add piquancy to dishes.

achar pickle. It is an essential part of an Indian meal, yet typically only small portions are eaten at a time. Vegetables and fruits are pickled in salt, spices and vinegar or oil, especially mustard oil. Meat, fish and nuts are pickled less commonly. There are many types of pickles and many regional variations. One of the most common pickles is *aam achar,* mango pickle, made with green mangoes. Because pickles keep well, they are a convenience food for travelers and are enjoyed with a variety of flatbreads.

ada bits of steamed rice flour paste used in the milk-based dessert called *ada payasam*. Flour and water are mixed together and spread on a banana leaf, which is rolled up and steamed over boiling water. When the paste is firm it is broken into bits.

adrak ginger. It usually is ground together with garlic and used as a paste.

ajmud (*Carum roxburgianum*) small seed used in chutneys, curries and pickles.

ajwain (ajowan) bishop's weed (*Carum ajowan*). The plant's small, ridged, brownish-green seeds, which taste like a more pungent type of thyme, are used in savory dishes, breads and snacks. Also called *omum*.

akhrot walnut; it is grown extensively in the valley of Kashmir in northern India. Ground nutmeats are used in desserts and for the production of oil.

alepak crystallized ginger.

aloo (alu) potato.

amb halad zedoary (*Curcuma zedoaria*), a rhizome closely related to turmeric, with thin, brown skin and yellow-orange flesh. It is used fresh or pickled.

ambadi type of hibiscus leaf; see *gongura*. Also called *kenaf*.

ambemohar round-grained variety of rice usually available only in India. It also is ground into flour.

amla Indian gooseberry (*Phyllanthus emblica*), a small, pale-yellow fruit with six vertical furrows, made into preserves, chutneys and a fermented drink.

amrood guava.

ananas pineapple.

anar pomegranate.

anardana pomegranate seed; used fresh or dried to provide tart flavor to dishes. Dried seeds are used whole or powdered.

anasphal star anise.

anda (aunda) egg.

angur grape.

anjur fig.

appalam thin, round, flat wafer made of lentils and spices, and ranging in diameter from about 2 to 8 inches. See *pappadam*. Also called *papad* (*paparh*).

arhar dal northern Indian name for a type of lentil with greenish skin and a yellow interior, which typically is sold split. Sometimes the lentils, known as pigeon peas, are coated with oil to extend their shelf life. Another name for this lentil is *toor* (*toorvar*) *dal*

aru peach.

arvi taro root (*Colocasia esculenta*).

arvi ka patta huge, heart-shaped leaf of the taro plant, which is cooked like chard. Also called *patra*.

ashti-madhu (madhuka) licorice; also called *pipli*.

atta wheat flour; also can be the generic name for flour.

bada big.

bada elaichi large cardamom with a dark brown pod and black seeds, which is used for rice and curry dishes. The spice is referred to as black cardamom.

badam almond.

baingan eggplant; also called *brinjal*.

bajri (bajra) millet; also called *kurakkan*. In the state of Gujarat, where millet is a staple grain, *bajri* is used to make a flat, griddle-cooked bread called *batloo*.

bakara (bakaro) ka gosht goat meat.

balchão Goan fish or shrimp "pickle," a hot paste traditionally made by grinding fish or shrimp with spices, palm vinegar, fermented palm sap and a flatbread containing dried shrimp. It is allowed to sit for a day or two before using in preparations of fish, seafood or meat. A recipe for shrimp *balchão* is on p. x.

bandhgohbi cabbage.

bangda mackerel.

barbatti green bean; also called *sem*.

barfi fudge. It is a popular sweet made with a variety of ingredients, including milk, sugar syrup, lentils, flour, nuts and coconut. Also spelled *burfi*.

basmati premier-quality, long-grained, aromatic rice grown primarily in the Himalayan foothills.

bataer quail.

batak duck.

batloo flat, griddle-cooked bread made of millet.

batti very dense, small, round roll made from wheat flour dough. When baked, the roll is pressed on top to crack open its crust, and melted clarified butter (*ghee*) is ladled over it. It is a specialty of Rajasthan.

battia griddle-cooked, thin, wheat bread bearing pinch marks made on its surface by the fingers. Fried bread is removed from the griddle, held over a flame to get small blackened spots on it and then crumpled by gentle squeezing. Melted butter (*ghee*) is poured over the bread. It is a specialty of Rajasthan.

batura type of fried bread made with all-purpose flour. It usually is served with a dish of spicy chickpeas (*chole*).

bawarchi cook, usually male.

bekti (bhekti) popular fish (*Lates calcarifer*) with firm, white, boneless flesh, which is found in the estuaries of Bengal. Fillets typically are fried or cooked in a curry. A larger fish also known as *bekti* in Bengal is actually a marine fish (*Protonibea diacantus*) of the croaker family, which is called *ghol* elsewhere.

belan short, wooden rolling pin used with the *chakla,* a board for rolling out bread dough.

ben (bhen) lotus root; also called *nedar.*

besale type of wild spinach, a regional specialty of Mangalore.

besan flour made from chickpeas (garbanzo beans) or from a variety of chickpea (gram *dal* or *chana dal*) that is usually sold split.

bhaji Maharashtrian name for vegetable. *Bhaji* also refers to a dish of vegetables stir-fried in spices and a little oil, producing a dish of dry (sauceless) consistency.

bhajia (bhajiya) vegetable fritter; vegetables are coated with chickpea flour batter and deep-fried. It more commonly is known as *pakora.*

bhakhar vadi Gujarati savory snack of small, flat, round pastries made from wheat and chickpea flour filled with a spiced potato stuffing.

bhakri chips.

bhakri roti Rajasthani flat, griddle-cooked bread made with sorghum. Also called *jowar bhakri.*

bhat cooked rice.

bheri mutton.

bheja brain.

bhindi okra.

bhunao sautéing or stir-frying ingredients with a small amount of liquid to extract the flavor. Cooking is complete when the mixture coalesces to form a mass and any fat that is present separates from it.

bhustrina lemon grass.

bhutha corn on the cob, which is available in the winter. It usually is grilled, husked, and rubbed with salt and sliced lime.

birshta carmelized onion.

bombil (bomil, boomla) milky-white, gelatinous-looking marine lizardfish (*Harpodon nehereus*) known as Bombay duck, which is particularly abundant in the seas around the seven islands comprising the city of Bombay (Mumbai) on the western coast of India. Bombay duck got its unusual name because locals likened its swimming behavior while seeking food near the surface of the water to a diving duck. The fish is most often eaten after it has been sun-dried. When eaten fresh, it typically is breaded and deep-fried.

bonda southern Indian round fritter.

boondi deep-fried chickpea flour droplets used as a snack or in a variety of dishes such as yogurt salad (*boondi raita*) and a round sweet (*ladoo*) enjoyed at special celebrations. See *Menu Guide*.

bori small blobs made from water-soaked lentils that are ground to a paste, mixed with spices and dried in the sun. They are fried in oil and added to stews or crumbled over vegetables. It is a traditional Bengali food.

boti boneless pieces of meat.

brinjal eggplant; also called *baingan*.

burfi fudge. It is a popular sweet made with a variety of ingredients, including milk, sugar syrup, lentils, flour, nuts and coconut. Also spelled *barfi*.

cachumber (kachumber) tangy salad made with a few raw vegetables, which are cut up, seasoned and dressed with a little oil or lemon juice.

chaap rib chop.

chaashni sugar-syrup.

chaat snack. A multitude of vendors sell an amazing array of savory and sweet snacks, prepared quickly to keep up with the competition.

chaat masala tangy spice mixture typically containing dried pomegranate seeds, powdered green mango, cumin, asafeotida (*hing*), cayenne, ginger and black rock salt. It is used to flavor street snacks, especially one made of potatoes.

chaaval (chawal) uncooked rice.

chaaval (chawal) ka atta rice flour.

chaaval (chawal) ke sev rice noodle.

chachinda snake gourd (*Trichosanthes cucumerina*), a long, curved, green vegetable eaten like zucchini squash; also spelled *chichinda*.

chakka jackfruit. It is eaten as a vegetable when unripe and as a fruit when ripe. Also called *kathal*.

chakla belan board and rolling pin used to roll out flatbreads such as *chappatis*. The *chakla* is a round (8- to 10-inch diameter) platform made from wood or marble, with 3 short pegs. Traditionally it is used on the ground. The *belan* is a short, wooden rolling pin.

chakotra grapefruit.

chakriphool star anise.

chaku knife.

chammach spoon.

chana chutney pungent relish made with chickpeas.

chana dal variety of chickpea that is matte yellow and usually sold split. It is slightly larger than the yellow lentil called *toorvar dal;* also called gram *dal.* Flour made from *chana dal* is called *besan,* as is flour made from another type of chickpea (garbanzo bean).

chandi ka varq (warq) very thin, edible silver foil, used to garnish or decorate food; also simply called *varq* (*warq*).

chappati tortilla-like, round, unleavened bread made with wheat flour and baked on an ungreased griddle. Also called *roti.*

charoli lentil-size, slightly flat, brown fruit kernel from a tree (*Buchanania latifolia*) of the cashew family. See *chirongi,* this *Guide.*

chas (chaas) buttermilk.

chatni (chutni) chutney, a pungent relish made from a blend of herbs, spices and a dominant fruit or vegetable. Also the name for sauce and ketchup.

chatpata spicy.

chaulai amaranth (*Amaranthus sp.*); the leaves are eaten as greens; also called *marsa.*

chewda (chevda) rice pounded flat. Also means a mixture of fried, savory snacks.

chhalni sieve.

chhana (chhanar) farmer's cheese; see *paneer.*

chichinda snake gourd (*Trichosanthes cucumerina*), a long, curved, green vegetable eaten like zucchini squash; also spelled *chachinda.*

chikoo sapota fruit.

chilgoza pine nut.

chilka peel.

chimta tongs.

China grass agar-agar, a vegetable substitute for gelatin obtained from seaweed (*Gelidium amansii*) and used to thicken puddings.

chingri Bengali word for shrimp.

chini sugar; also called *shakkar.*

chirongi lentil-size, slightly flat, round, brown fruit kernel from a tree (*Buchanania latifolia*) of the cashew family, primarily used to garnish cakes, puddings and *halva* (*halwa*); also called *charoli.*

chole chickpea (garbanzo bean); also the name of a vegetable dish made with chickpeas.

choliya unripe chickpea.

chor magaz melon seed. The seeds are added to several curries, snacks and desserts. They are also ground and used to thicken dishes.

chota elaichi green cardamom.

chow-chow chayote squash, a pear-shaped vegetable with thin green skin and crunchy white pulp.

chowli black-eyed pea; also called *lobhia*.

chuara date; also called *khajur*.

chukandari beet.

chundakai slightly bitter, marble-size, smooth-skinned, round gourd used for soups, pickles, curries and ritual food (*prasad*) offered to a deity before it is eaten.

chutni (chatni) chutney, a pungent relish. See *chatni*.

copra dried coconut meat.

copra ka tel coconut oil.

curd plain yogurt. Also called *dahi*.

curry see *kari*.

daana (dana) seed.

dahi plain yogurt; also called curd. Indian yogurt is thick, creamy and firm.

dahi chappati unleavened, griddle-baked, round bread (*chappati*) made with a yogurt-enriched wheat flour dough.

dakor gota instant fritter mix containing chickpea and wheat flours, coriander, red chile pepper, turmeric and asafoetida (*hing*).

dakshini term found in restaurants indicating that food from southern India is on the menu.

dal legume (lentil, pea or bean).

dal gosht meat cooked in *dal* (lentils).

dalchini cinnamon.

dalia cracked wheat; also the name of a breakfast porridge made of cracked wheat. Another name for cracked wheat is *lapsi*.

dalna coarsely ground.

degchi metallic, handle-less cooking pot.

deghi mirch paprika made from the Kashmiri red chile pepper, which is used primarily for color.

desi gajar native black carrot.

desi ghee pure, clarified butter. It is made by heating butter until its water evaporates and its milk solids (proteins), which settle on the bottom of the pan, darken slightly. The butterfat is then strained to remove the milk solids. Also simply called *ghee.*

dhaaba roadside eatery. Initially these eateries existed for truckdrivers. They are known for simple but fresh meals.

dhakai parota elaborate version of *parota,* the flat, unleavened and usually triangular-shaped bread made of wheat flour and clarified butter (*ghee*). The *dhakai parota* is large, multilayered, circular and a specialty of Bengal enjoyed with curries. Elsewhere the *parota* is called *paratha.*

dhaniya coriander. It is the name for both seed and leaf (cilantro); the leaf is also called *hari dhaniya* and *kothmir.*

dhungar process of smoking food at the end of cooking. Smoke is created by placing clarified butter (*ghee*) on a burning coal, often topped with a clove. The coal is put in the center of a bowl containing the food, typically set on a small, overturned metal dish, and the bowl is covered to allow the smoke generated to flavor the food within.

Diwali Festival of Lights, an important Hindu holiday associated with feasting, social gatherings and the exchange of food (fruits and sweets). It is celebrated throughout India and in Indian communities around the world. Diwali is as significant to Hindus as Christmas is to Christians.

doodh milk.

doodhi bottle gourd; a light green, smooth-skinned vegetable resembling a stubby baseball bat. Also called *ghiya* and *lauki.*

dubble roti loaf of bread leavened with yeast, introduced to India by the Europeans (Portuguese, Dutch, British and French).

dum meat steamed meat.

dum pukht cooking process whereby food steams in its own juices, traditionally over a low charcoal fire. To accomplish this, the cooking pan and its lid are sealed together with a putty-like strip of dough (*dum*) made of flour.

elaichi cardamom. The variety with large, dark-brown pods is called *bada elaichi;* the variety with small green pods is called *chota elaichi.*

farsan Gujarati fried snack largely based on beans and lentils. It is an ingredient of snack mixtures called *chewda* (*chevda*).

foogath southern Indian dish of leftovers turned into a dry (gravyless) dish.

fryum name for chips or fried snack items in Chennai.

gai ka gosht beef.

gajar carrot.

garam masala ground spice mixture usually containing cinnamon, cardamom, cloves, cumin, black peppercorns and bay leaves.

gehu (gehun) wheat kernel or berry.

gehun phulka type of *chappati* made from dough containing soaked and ground wheat berries, buttermilk and clarified butter, in addition to wheat flour, and rolled paper-thin.

ghee clarified butter; see *desi ghee.*

ghiya bottle gourd; see *doodhi.*

ghol large marine fish (*Protonibea diacantus*) of the croaker family; see *bekti.*

ghosala ridged gourd (*Luffa acutangula*) bearing ten longitudinal ridges and a tapered neck. Young gourds are sliced and cooked as a vegetable, which tastes similar to zucchini. Also called *tori* and *kali tori.*

gilas glass.

goda masala black ground-spice mixture from the state of Maharastra typically made with cardamom, cinnamon sticks, whole cloves, bay leaves, sesame seeds, coriander seeds, and flaked coconut. The coconut is dry-roasted until dark, giving the spice mixture its characteristic black color.

gohbi cauliflower. Also called *phool gohbi.*

gongura type of hibiscus (*Hibiscus cannabinus*). The leaves of the plant are used to make pickles and chutneys in southern India. A popular curry in the state of Andhra Pradesh is made with the leaves cooked with sliced onions. Other names for this plant are *ambadi* and *kenaf.*

gosht meat. Also called *maas.*

gram certain plants such as beans and chickpeas, or their seeds. Indians use this English word in the names of several of their varieties of *dal* (legumes).

gram dal matte yellow variety of split chickpea that is slightly larger than the yellow lentil; also called *chana dal.* Flour made from gram *dal* is called *besan,* as is flour made from chickpeas (garbanzo beans). Usage of the English word gram, which means the plant or seeds from certain plants such as beans and chickpeas, can be confusing.

guar phali cluster bean (*Cyamopsis tetragonoloba*). The slim, bright-green pods have a pointed end and grow in small groups. Both young pods and mature seeds are eaten as a vegetable. Seeds are also the source of a gum (guar) used as an emulsifier and thickener in food products.

guchchi morel.

gulab rose.

gulabi China grass rose-flavored gelatin made with agar-agar (China grass).

gulabjal rose water.

gulkhand rose petal jam.

gur (gul) raw, unprocessed sugar made from sugar cane juice or palm juice; also called *jaggery*.

gurda kidney.

hak thick-leaved green vegetable that grows year round in Kashmir.

haldi turmeric.

halka moderately hot; mild. Also means a light meal.

halva (halwa) sweet made from a variety of mixtures, including lentils, grains, seeds, vegetables and fruits.

hamam dasta mortar and pestle used for grinding spices.

handi round, handle-less cooking pot with a wok-like bottom and a narrow opening on top. It is used for slow-cooking food in steam.

hanuman phal cherimoya (*Annona cherimola/cherimoya*), an oval to heart-shaped green fruit, 4 to 8 inches long, with a variable surface pattern of either small bumps or indentations resembling thumbprints. The white, buttery pulp is sweet and juicy.

hari green.

hari dhaniya cilantro; also simply called *dhaniya*. Another word for cilantro is *kothmir*.

hari mirch green chile pepper.

hilsa silvery, fatty shad (*Tenualosa ilisha*) favored by Bengalis. Young fish are caught in rivers as they migrate to sea water, and mature fish are caught when they migrate up rivers to spawn in fresh water. Called *illisher* in Bengali.

hing asafoetida, a strong, sulfur-smelling, milky gum resin from mature roots of a member of the giant fennel family (*Ferula foetida*) grown in Kashmir. Small amounts of powdered resin are used to enhance the flavor of dishes.

illisher Bengali name for the silvery, fatty shad (*Tenualosa ilisha*). See entry under Hindi word for this fish, *hilsa*.

imli tamarind, a pod-like fruit about 4 inches long with a thin brown shell surrounding sour, sticky, red-brown pulp used as a souring agent.

imli ki rus tamarind water made by soaking tamarind pulp in warm water and used to add piquancy to dishes.

ittar essence, usually of flowers such as the rose, which is used in cookery. Other commonly used essences are screwpine (*kewra*) and a very fragrant grass called *khus*.

jaee oats.

jaggery unprocessed sugar produced from sugar cane juice or palm juice; also called *gur.*

jaiphal nutmeg.

jamikand (zamikand) elephant-foot yam (*Amorphophallus campanulatus*); also called *suran.*

jamun star apple; small, purple-skinned fruit (*Chrysophyllum cainito*) having eight white segments, each housing a flattened, brown seed.

jardaloo apricot; also called *khubani.*

javitri mace.

jeera cumin.

jheenga (jhinga) shrimp.

josh term indicating that a dish has body heat-inducing spices. See *rogan josh, Menu Guide.*

jowar sorghum.

jowar bhakri Rajasthani flat, griddle-cooked bread made with sorghum. Also called *bhakri roti.*

jumrool water apple (*Syzygium samarangense*), a pear-shaped fruit with waxy skin and crispy, juicy flesh. It is a good thirst quencher.

jungli wild.

jungli amba ambarella, an oblong fruit (*Spondias pinnata*), yellow when ripe, with a flavor and fragrance resembling pineapple.

jungli dalchini cassia; used like cinnamon in savory dishes. Peppery-tasting, dried cassia flower buds sometimes are used to fasten together betel leaf packets (*paan*) filled with spices, seeds and chopped betel nuts. The packets, or quids, are chewed postprandially as a digestive aid, stimulant and mouth freshener.

kababchini (kebabchini) allspice.

kabuli chana dried chickpea (garbanzo bean).

kachori deep-fried bread containing a savory filling.

kachri variety of cucumber about 2 inches long that is dried, ground to a powder and used as a meat tenderizer and souring agent.

kachumber (cachumber) tangy salad made with a few raw vegetables, which are cut up, seasoned and dressed with a little oil or lemon juice.

kaddu pumpkin.

kaddu kas grater.

kadhai (karai) two-handled frying and serving pot resembling a shallow wok with a rounder, flatter bottom.

kagzi nibu lime; also simply called *nibu.*

kair small, berry-like fruit grown on a leafless, thorny tree in arid regions of the state of Rajasthan. It typically is eaten with two other desert foods: a bean pod (*sangri*) that grows on a different thorny tree and another desert food called *kumita*. The dish combining these ingredients is aptly called *kair sangri kumita* (see *Menu Guide*). Despite the importance of sun-dried or pickled *kair* as survival food, the fruits also are eaten fresh. Also spelled *kher.*

kairi unripe mango used for cooking.

kaith plum-size, whitish-gray fruit (*Feronia limonia*; syn. *Limonia acidisima*) called wood apple and elephant apple. Its brown, sticky, aromatic pulp, full of tiny white seeds, is enclosed in a tough, woody shell about ¼-inch thick that requires a hammer to crack open. The pulp is eaten raw or used in chutneys, beverages and ice cream. Also called *kapittha.*

kaju cashew nut.

kakari (kakdi) variety of cucumber enjoyed in salads. This light-green, crunchy vegetable with a ridged surface is about 1 inch in diameter and 1 foot long.

kala (kali) black.

kala chana black chickpea (garbanzo bean).

kala jeera black cumin seeds (*Cuminum cyminum*); also called *shah jeera.*

kala namak black (actually grayish-pink) mineral salt with a distinctive flavor used to enhance the taste of certain salads, snacks, beverages and chutneys; also called *saindhav.*

kalan mushroom; also called *khumbi.*

kaleja liver.

kali mirch black pepper.

kali tori ridged gourd; see *ghosala.*

kalonji small, flat, oblong black seed (*Nigella sativa*) known as nigella, black caraway, and black onion seed. See *klonji.*

kalpasi lichen used as an herb. It is found on cinnamon trees or on trees near the seashore during the monsoon.

kamal kakri lotus stem.

kamrakh starfruit.

kanchkola unripe (green) banana.

kane ladyfish (*Elops saurus*), a small, silvery, bony freshwater fish considered a delicacy in the coastal city of Mangalore in the state of Karnataka.

kanji liquid left after boiling rice in excess water; bland nourishment for invalids.

kapittha wood apple or elephant apple; see *kaith.*

karchchi ladle.

karela bitter gourd; it looks like a ridged cucumber covered with warts.

kari word in Tamil (south Indian language) for black pepper, which became associated with a dish of vegetables with spices. Ultimately it became synonymous with Indian food to the English, who used the spelling curry. To Indians, curry has come to mean a sauce or gravy.

kari patta (patha) curry leaf (*Murraya koenigii*); also called *meetha neem.*

karimeen silver fish (*Etroplus suratensis*) with vertical black stripes found in the brackish backwaters of the southern state of Kerala, where it is considered a delicacy.

karva bitter.

Kasmiri deghi mirch mild red pepper used primarily for color.

kasoori (kasthuri) methi dried fenugreek leaves.

kata fork.

kathal jackfruit; also called *chakka.*

katla fleshy, freshwater carp (*Catla catla*) especially prized in Bengal.

katori small metal bowl for serving dishes with gravy or *dal,* usually served as part of an extensive meal with several other similar bowls on a metal *thali,* a circular tray with a shallow rim. See *thali.*

kebabchini (kababchini) allspice.

keema (kheema) minced meat.

kekra crab.

kela banana.

kela ka fool banana blossom.

kenaf type of hibiscus leaf; see *gongura.* Also called *ambadi.*

kesar saffron; it is grown in the valley of Kashmir in northern India; also called *zaafraan.*

kesar kasturi alcoholic drink made of saffron.

kewra (keora) essence (*ittar*) extracted from the flower of the screwpine (*Pandanus sp.*), used to flavor certain foods.

khajur date; also called *chuara.*

khane ka soda baking soda.

kharbooja cantelope.

khasta tender.

khatta sour.

khatta mitha sweet-sour.

kheema minced meat, normally lamb.

kheera cucumber.

kher small, berry-like fruit grown on a tree in arid regions of the state of Rajasthan. See entry under alternative spelling *kair.*

khichri mixture; also means a dish of lentils, rice and spices. The British added fish to the dish and spelled it *kedgeree.*

khoya milk reduced by cooking until a thick, ricotta-like residue remains; also called *mawa;* also spelled *koya.*

khubani apricot; also called *jardaloo.*

khumbi mushroom; also called *kalan.*

khus fragrant grass (*Vetivaria sp.*) made into an essence (*ittar*) used in cookery to flavor certain beverages and sweets.

khus-khus poppy seed.

kishmish blond raisin made from white grapes; the dark-brown raisin, which is larger, is called *manukka.* Generally, blond raisins are used in Indian cookery.

klonji small, flat, oblong black seed known as nigella, black caraway and black onion seed. One end of the seed is sharply pointed. It is one of the five ingredients comprising the popular Bengali spice blend called *panch phoron;* also spelled *kalonji.*

kofta deep-fried ground meat or vegetable ball, usually served in gravy.

kokum (kokam) red mango (*Garcinia indica*), relative of the mangosteen, which is native to the western coastal regions of southern India. The fruit is dark purple when ripe. Its rind is dried, becoming dark black, and used as a flavorant and souring agent. Food containing *kokum* becomes somewhat pinkish-purple.

korma dish with thick gravy or sauce; also spelled *kurma* and *qorma.*

kothmir cilantro. Also called *dhaniya* and *hari dhaniya.*

koya milk reduced by cooking until a thick, ricotta-like residue remains; also called *mawa;* also spelled *khoya.*

kulcha type of flatbread similar to *naan,* made from leavened, white flour dough, but it is kneaded with more clarified butter (*ghee*). *Kulcha* can be plain or stuffed with various fillings.

kulfi Indian ice cream traditionally made with milk that has been reduced and concentrated by boiling (*khoya*). Condensed milk is used a quick substitute. *Kulfi* typically is frozen in individual conical, metal containers with lids.

kulith horse gram (*Macrotyloma uniflorum*), a small, flat, shiny red to brown lentil.

kumita bean pod grown in arid regions of the state of Rajasthan. It typically is eaten in combination with two other desert foods—a bean pod (*sangri*) and a small, berry-like fruit called *kair* (*kher*)—in a dish called *kair sangri kumita.* See *Menu Guide.*

kurakkan millet; see *bajri.*

kurma dish with thick gravy or sauce; also spelled *korma.*

kurmura puffed rice. It is a prominent ingredient in many snacks. Also called *mamra.*

kursi chair.

kuthari red rice grown in Kerala.

lahsun garlic.

lahsun ki chutney hot garlic relish.

lal red.

lal mirchi dried red chile pepper.

lapsi cracked wheat; it is used to make porridge and some snacks. Another name for cracked wheat is *dalia.*

lassi yogurt-based drink that can be sweet or salty and have any number of flavor variations.

lauki bottle gourd; also spelled *louki.* Another word for bottle gourd is *doodhi.*

laung clove.

limboo na phool citric acid powder or crystals used to provide tartness without adding moisture, which is necessary for dried preparations such as spicy snack mixtures made with cereals, lentils and nuts. See *chewda* (*chevda*), *Menu Guide.*

lobhia black-eyed peas; also called *chowli.*

louki bottle gourd; also spelled *lauki.* Another word for bottle gourd is *doodhi.*

luchi Bengali deep-fried bread made from wheat flour and clarified butter (*ghee*). Circles are cut out of thinly rolled dough and fried in oil. The bread puffs up like a balloon, hastened by spooning hot oil over the top of it. In other parts of the country this bread is called *puri.*

maas meat. Also called *gosht.*

maas ka sula pieces of meat grilled on a skewer. Minced meat grilled on a skewer is called *seekh kabab* or *kakori kabab.*

machi (machli) fish; also called *meen.*

mahseer prized freshwater fish (*Tor spp.*) of the carp family.

maida all-purpose flour.

makhana puffed lotus seed.

makhanphal avocado.

makka (makki) corn.

makkhan butter.

makki ka atta corn flour.

makki ki roti griddle-cooked flatbread made of freshly-ground corn flour, which is eaten in rural areas of northern India during the winter. It is served with daubs of clarified butter (*ghee*) on top.

malai cream formed on top of whole milk that has been heated and allowed to cool slowly at room temperature.

malta citrus fruit resembling the lemon, with mottled green and yellow skin and sweet juice. Also called *mausami.*

mamra puffed rice. It is a prominent ingredient in many snacks. Also called *kurmura.*

mangori dried, water-based paste popular in the state of Rajasthan that is available in the markets in several forms. Considered survival food, it is made from ground yellow chickpeas (*chana dal*) and paprika, sometimes flavored with asafoetida (*hing*).

manguskai mangosteen (*Garcinia mangostana*), a plum-size fruit with thick, dark-red to purple rind and delicious segmented white pulp.

manukka dark-brown raisin; a blond raisin, made from a white grape, is called *kishmish.*

marati muka narrow, elongated, cardamom-like pod used in Hyderabad to flavor a *biryani,* an elaborate dish made with lamb, chicken, vegetables, or even fish, cooked with saffron-flavored rice. See *Menu Guide.*

marsa amaranth (*Amaranthus sp.*); the leaves are eaten as greens. Also called *chaulai.*

masala generic term for spice mixture.

masala dani metal spice box with an airtight lid. The box holds several small open bowls arranged in a circle around the inner edge, each containing a different spice.

masaledar with spices.

masoor dal split red lentil.

matar fresh or dried pea.

matki moth bean (*Vigna aconitifolia*). The short pods are eaten as a vegetable, and the seeds, which are the size of rice grains, are used whole or split.

mausami citrus fruit resembling the lemon, with mottled green and yellow skin and sweet juice. Also called *malta.*

mawa milk reduced by cooking until a thick, ricotta-like residue remains; also called *khoya* (*koya*).

meen fish; also called *machi* (*machli*).

meetha neem curry leaf (*Murraya koenigii*); also called *kari patta* (*patha*).

methi fenugreek. It is the name for the leaves and stony, yellow-brown seeds of the plant, both of which are edible. Fresh leaves are eaten as a vegetable; dry leaves (*kasoori methi*) are used as an herb.

methi roti griddle-cooked flatbread containing chopped fenugreek.

mez table.

mirch (mirchi) red or green chile pepper.

mishri small pieces of crystallized sugar.

mishri mawa sweetened, reduced milk.

missi roti round, griddle-cooked flatbread made from chickpeas and wheat flour. Onions, fenugreek seeds, cumin seeds, pomegranate seeds and spinach are a few of the ingredients that can be added to the dough.

mitha (mithi) sweet.

mithai sweets.

mithai paratha triangle-shaped, multi-layered flatbread stuffed with a sweet filling. See *paratha,* this *Guide.*

molee (mole) dish cooked in a coconut milk sauce and associated with southern India.

mooli daikon radish.

moong (mung) dal yellow, split mung bean. Whole mung beans sometimes are called green gram.

moongphali peanut.

moongphali ka tel peanut oil; it is used in southern Indian cookery.

moori puffed rice.

moti roti round, griddle-fried flatbread made with yogurt-based, all-purpose flour dough. The breads are chewy and slightly sour.

mowal edible extract made by boiling cockscomb flowers, which is used as a red colorant in certain Kashmiri Muslim dishes.

murabha sweet, vegetable or fruit preserve.

murel fish (*Chana striata*) commonly known as striped snakehead, whose almost boneless, firm, white flesh is prized in some parts of India.

murgh (murgha) chicken; colored ones are free-running and eat natural foods. Their meat is considered tastier than that of white birds, which are caged and fed feed.

muru oyster; also called *shukti.*

muruggai drumstick, a green bean-like pod eaten as a vegetable. See *sahan.*

murukku southern Indian savory snack made from rice flour. Batter is extruded in the form of circles from a special mold and deep-fried until golden.

naan flat, leavened, white flour bread with a crispy crust, which is baked in a coal or wood-fired clay oven (*tandoor*). The dough is enriched with yogurt, eggs and clarified butter (*ghee*). *Naan* traditionally has a tear-drop shape. One way to get this shape is to slap a round ball of dough into a flattened, oblong shape with the palms of the hands. By holding on to one end of the flattened dough, its weight stretches the held end into a point. Fennel seeds or nigella seeds sometimes are sprinkled on top of the bread before it is baked. *Naan* is eaten plain or stuffed with various fillings.

naan khatai cardamom-flavored, slightly sweet biscuit or cookie topped with bits of pistachios. A tiny amount of ammonium carbonate is added to the dough to make the top crinkly.

namak salt.

namkeen savory; salty. *Namkeen* also means savory snacks.

naram soft.

nariyal coconut.

nariyal ka doodh coconut milk.

nashpati pear.

navratan mixed vegetables.

nedar lotus root; also called *ben*.

nendra kai type of banana grown in Kerala, which is cooked and used to make the classic sweet called *kaiadai* (see *Menu Guide*).

nibu (nimbu) lemon or lime; another word for lime is *kagzi nibu* (*nimbu*).

omum bishop's weed. See *ajwain*.

ondhwa blend of rice and chickpea flour (*besan*) used to make a Gujarati savory dish called *handvo* (see *Menu Guide*).

paan betel leaf packets with a variety of fillings including spices, seeds, sweet preserves, tobacco and chopped betel nuts. The packets, or quids, are chewed postprandially as a digestive aid, stimulant and mouth freshener. Habitual usage of *paan* is similar to tobacco chewing. Also see *supari,* this *Guide*.

paan ka patta leaf of a pepper-like plant used to make the packets (*paan*) that are chewed postprandially. See *paan,* this *Guide*.

pakora vegetable fritter; vegetables are coated with chickpea flour batter and deep-fried. Also known as *bhajia* (*bhajiya*).

palak spinach.

panch phoron colorful, aromatic Bengali spice mixture containing five ingredients used whole or ground, and mixed in equal proportions: black mustard seeds, fennel seeds, fenugreek seeds, cumin seeds and black nigella seeds (*klonji*), also identified as black caraway and black onion seed. This spice blend gives Bengali cuisine its characteristic aroma.

paneer (panir) farmer's cheese made by curdling boiled milk with vinegar or fresh lemon juice. The white curds formed (*paneer*) are strained to remove the whey (which can be used in other dishes) and flattened under a weight for a few hours to draw out excess whey and set the cheese. The Bengali name for this cheese is *chhana* (*chhanar*).

pani water.

pani-puri smaller version of ordinary *puri,* which is used to make a street snack. It is a deep-fried, crispy bread made from wheat flour and clarified butter (*ghee*), which puffs up like a balloon in hot oil. Its top is broken off, and a mixture of spices in water (*pani*) is spooned into the puri. Pani-puri is best eaten in a single bite.

papad (paparh) very thin, round wafer made with lentils and spices. See *pappadam.*

papadi hyacinth bean (*Lablab purpurus*). The immature pods and their seeds are eaten.

papita (papitha; papeetha) papaya; the Bengali word for this fruit is *peper* (*pepey*).

pappadam very thin, round wafer, ranging in diameter from about 2 to 8 inches, which is made with lentils and spices. Flame-roasted or deep-fried, it is eaten as a snack or accompanying a meal, like chips. Also called *papad, paparh,* and *appalam.*

parat round, shallow tray for kneading dough.

paratha griddle-fried, unleavened, flatbread made from wheat flour and clarified butter (*ghee*). The triangular-shaped bread is multi-layered. It can also be stuffed. When *paratha* is stuffed, it often is made round because this shape is easier to stuff. In Bengal it is called *parota;* also see *dhakai parota,* this *Guide.*

parval (parwal) pointed gourd (*Trichosanthes dioica*)—a green, striped vegetable that grows in various sizes and shapes. It is cooked alone or with other vegetables and meat. The Bengali name for pointed gourd is *patol.*

patna type of long-grain rice grown in northern India and enjoyed daily. The grains are milky white and have a mild taste. It is also made into flour. A red-husked variety (red *patna*) grown in central and western India is considered a regional rice and consumed locally.

patra taro leaf. Also called *arvi ka patta.*

pau small, soft bread loaf typically accompanying a dish of bread and vegetables called *pau bhaji.* The dish is a popular street snack in Mumbai (Bombay) and Gujarat.

pauni perforated frying spoon.

pavta lima bean.

pawa flattened, flaky rice. See *poha,* this *Guide.*

peeli yellow.

peeli mirch yellow chile pepper.

peper (pepey) papaya; see *papita,* this *Guide.*

petha ash gourd (*Benincasa hispida*), a white-fleshed gourd with pale-green skin. Pieces are crystallized to make a candied confection of the same name, which is a specialty of Agra in the state of Uttar Pradesh.

peyaz onion; also spelled *piyaz.*

phal fruit.

phool gohbi cauliflower. Also simply called *gohbi.*

phulka type of *chappati,* a round, griddle-cooked, flatbread made of wheat flour. It is puffy on one side because that side of the bread is undercooked on the griddle and then held over an open flame, which not only causes steam to puff it up on the flamed side, but completes the cooking process. The finished product is hollow with a thicker layer on the bottom and a thin layer on top.

pillau (pulau) (rice) pilaf.

pipli licorice; also called *ashti-madhu* (*madhuka*).

pista pistachio nut.

piyaz onion; also spelled *peyaz.*

podhina mint; also spelled *pudhina.*

poha flattened, flaky rice made out of cheaper rice. The rice is parboiled and flattened by rollers until wafer-thin. *Poha* is used to make snacks, sweets and cereals. Also called *pawa.*

poori deep-fried bread; see *puri.*

poriyal Tamil name for a dry (sauceless) vegetable preparation containing grated coconut. It is a regional dish of southern India. In Kerala the dish is called *thoran.*

prasad what food is called after it has been offered to a deity; it usually is eaten as part of a religious ritual.

pudhina mint; also spelled *podhina.*

pudla spicy pancake with grated vegetables.

Punjabi tinda baby Indian pumpkin; see *tinda*, this *Guide.*

puran poli *chappati* filled with a sweet stuffing made from a type of yellow split lentil (*toor dal*), raw cane or palm sugar (*jaggery*) and cardamom, which is shallow-fried in clarified butter (*ghee*). This sweet bread usually is made for special occasions.

puri deep-fried bread made from wheat flour and clarified butter (*ghee*). Circles are cut out of thinly rolled dough and fried in oil. The bread puffs up like a balloon, hastened by spooning hot oil over the top of it. In Bengal this bread is called *luchi.* Also spelled *poori.*

pyala cup.

qorma dish with thick gravy or sauce; also spelled *korma* (*kurma*).

rai mustard seed; Indian cookery uses black mustard seeds; also called *sarso daana* (*dana*).

raji red millet.

rajma red kidney bean. Also the name of a dish made with this bean. See *Menu Guide.*

ras juice.

rava (rawa) semolina; also called *sooji.*

rawas Indian white salmon, a firm-fleshed fish similar to the sea bass.

roghani naan a type of *naan* (leavened, flat, white-flour bread) made red by brushing it with saffron water before it is baked in a clay oven (*tandoor*).

rohu variety of carp.

roomali roti handkerchief bread—a large, thin (as thin as a handkerchief), pliable circle (about 16 inches in diameter) cooked on a convex griddle. Also spelled *rumali roti.*

roti tortilla-like, round, unleavened bread made with wheat flour and baked on an ungreased griddle. Also called *chappati.*

rotla griddle-fried, round, flatbread made from millet flour called *bajri;* thicker than a *chappati.*

saag cooked (puréed) vegetables.

sabudana name for both tapioca, a starch from cassava (*manioc; Manihot utilissima*), and sago, a starch extracted from the sago palm (*Metroxylon sagu*).

sabut whole.

sada plain.

safed white.

safed mirch white pepper.

sahan (sahjan) drumstick, a green, bean-like pod from a drought-tolerant tree (*Moringa oleifera*), eaten as a vegetable when immature. The thin layer of pulp around the seeds of the pod is eaten. Pods typically are cut into pieces about 2 inches long and cooked. Also called *muruggai.*

saindhav black (actually grayish-pink) mineral salt. See *kala namak,* this *Guide.*

samosa crispy, deep-fried, triangular pastries stuffed with meat or vegetables; called *singhara* in Bengal.

sangri bean pod grown in arid regions of the state of Rajasthan. It typically is eaten with two other desert foods—a bean pod (*kumita*) and a small, berry-like fruit called *kair* (*kher*)—in a dish called *kair sangri kumita* (see *Menu Guide*).

santh pickled boar meat.

sarso mustard greens eaten as a vegetable.

sarso daana (dana) mustard seed; Indian cookery uses black mustard seeds; also called *rai*.

sarso ka tel mustard oil.

sauf (saunf) fennel seed.

seb apple.

seekh skewer with a wider than usual diameter (3/8 inch) for grilling special minced meat kebabs. See *seekh kebab, Menu Guide*.

seetha phal sugar apple (*Annona squamosa*), a round to ovoid green fruit up to 4 inches long, with many small bumps studding the surface, and sweet, white segmented pulp. Also called *sharifa* and *sitaphal*.

sella parboiled Basmati rice.

sem green bean; also called *barbatti*.

sev crispy, deep-fried vermicelli made with chickpea flour (*besan*), usually eaten as a snack or as part of a snack.

sevian ultra-thin, wheat-flour vermicelli used to make milk pudding.

shah jeera black cumin seed (*Cuminum cyminum*); also called *kala jeera*.

shahad (shaid) honey.

shak Gujarati word for vegetable. *Shak* also refers to the Gujarati way of stir-frying vegetables in spices and a little oil, producing a dish of dry (sauceless) consistency.

shakarkand sweet potato.

shakkar sugar; also called *chini*.

shalgam turnip.

sharaab alcohol.

sharifa sugar apple (*Annona squamosa*). See *seetha phal,* this *Guide*.

sheermal sweet, round, leavened, flatbread made from all-purpose flour, eggs, milk, sugar and clarified butter (*ghee*). It traditionally is baked in a clay oven (*tandoor*) until brown spots appear, then removed and basted in a saffron-milk solution, which turns the bread a rich yellowish-orange color, before being baked a few minutes more. Sometimes melted *ghee* is brushed on the baked bread.

sherbet refreshing, flavored drink. A common one is flavored with rose water.

shorba soup; broth.

shukti oyster; also called *muru*.

sil batta traditional, two-piece, stone utensil used for grinding spices. Spices are ground on a flat platform (*sil*) with a handle-less cylinder resembling a rolling pin (*batta*).

simla mirch bell pepper.

singhara Bengali term for *samosa,* a crispy, deep-fried, triangular pastry stuffed with meat or vegetables; also the Hindi term for water chestnut.

sippee clam.

sirka vinegar.

sitaphal sugar apple (*Annona squamosa*). See *seetha phal,* this *Guide*. In northern India, *sitaphal* refers to a type of gourd with red-orange flesh.

siya jeera caraway.

sone ka varq (warq) paper-thin, edible, 24-carat gold sheet used to decorate certain foods. Also simply called *varq* (*warq*).

sonth sweet and sour sauce made from tamarind. It also is the name for dried ginger.

sooji semolina; also called *rava* (*rawa*).

sowa (soya, sua) dill.

subja tiny black seeds from a particular variety of basil. Dried seeds are placed in water, which causes them to swell and become gelatinous on the surface. They are used in the chilled milk drink called *falooda* (see *Menu Guide*).

subji Hindi word for vegetable. *Subji* also refers to a dish of vegetables cooked in spices and a little oil, producing a dish of dry (sauceless) consistency.

sukha dry.

sukha bhuna jeera dark-brown, dry-roasted cumin.

sula skewer. A special, thicker skewer (*seekh*) is used for minced meat kebabs (*seekh kebabs;* see *Menu Guide*).

supari areca nut, commonly called the betel nut, the woody, astringent seed of the areca palm tree (*Areca catechu*). The hard, light-brown nut has a variegated interior. Pieces or slices of the nut are part of a mixture, which can include spices, seeds, sweet jam, sugar and lime, that is wrapped up in a leaf (from a pepper-like plant) and chewed postprandially as a digestive aid, stimulant and breath freshener. The lime in the leaf packet (*paan*) helps the stimulatory chemicals of the nut get into the bloodstream.

suran elephant-foot yam (*Amorphophallus campanulatus*); also called *jamikand* (*zamikand*).

surti kolam variety of short grain rice grown in south Gujarat.

tadka tempering, a seasoning method of frying spices in hot oil before adding them to a dish.

tak-a-tak term refering to the sound a metal spatula makes when it hits the side of a pan. It is used in the names of some dishes cooked on a griddle.

tamater tomato.

tandoor clay oven used to bake flatbreads such as *naan*. Rolled *naan* dough is slapped onto the oven wall to bake. Long metal skewers are used to remove cooked bread from the oven wall. *Tandoori*-cooked food is a northern Indian specialty.

tandoori masala hot, bright-red spice blend containing cayenne pepper, ground cumin and coriander seeds, reddened with a few drops of food coloring. It is added to marinades or hot oil, and imparts flavor and a dark orange color to foods as they bake, traditionally in a *tandoori* oven.

tarbuj watermelon.

tarka cooking process of seasoning (tempering) a dish with hot oil and spices after it is cooked.

tarkari Punjabi name for vegetable. In Punjab *tarkari* also refers to a dish of stir-fried vegetables in spices and a little oil, producing a dish of dry (sauceless) consistency.

taute thick-skinned, sweet, yellow cucumber used to make dishes like *sambhar,* a southern Indian dish of lentils (*dal*) with vegetables. *Taute* turns black when touched, so it is stored suspended from ceilings by palm fronds.

tava slightly concave iron griddle used to fry breads such as *chappatis* and *parathas*.

taza fresh.

teesiriya mussel.

tej patha (patta) bay leaf.

tel oil.

tendli gherkin.

tez hot; spicy; sharp.

thali term for a "plate" meal served in small metal bowls (*katori*) placed close to the edge of a short-rimmed metal plate, as well as the name of the plate itself. Sometimes plates have small indentations that serve as bowls. Each bowl holds a different dish. The extensive repast includes several vegetarian or meat curry dishes, relishes, yogurt, and one or more desserts, which typically are in bowls on the right side of the tray. Rice is heaped in the center of the tray, along with some round, flatbreads such as *chappati, puri* or *roti,* and *pappadam* wafers. The *thali* is a southern Indian contribution to Indian cookery, but this type of meal also is available in the north. In the south, a more common plate is a large banana leaf.

thandai cooling milk-based drink made with a paste of ground seeds, nuts and spices.

thoran (thoren) Malayalam name for a sauceless, stir-fried vegetable dish with coconut from the state of Kerala. The Tamil name for this dish is *poriyal*.

tikha spicy.

tikka (tikki) generic name for patties or small pieces of meat or farmer's cheese (*paneer*), sometimes grilled on skewers.

tikkar roti griddle-fried, round, flatbread made from a mixture of whole-wheat and corn flours. Thicker than usual flatbreads, *tikkar roti* also contains chopped tomato, onion, green chile pepper and cilantro. It is a Rajasthani favorite.

tikki fried patty of mashed vegetables or meat; also part of a street snack (*chaat*) consisting of a patty of mashed potatoes with spices.

til sesame.

til ka tel sesame oil.

tinda baby Indian squash (*Citrullus vulgaris,* var. *fistulosus*)—a bright-green, round, tomato-sized vegetable; also called Punjabi *tinda*.

tirphal Sichuan pepper, the berry of the prickly ash tree (*Zanthoxylum rhetsa*), which grows in western India. Used crushed, the berries provide a spicy, woody taste (not hot) and general numbness to the mouth. They are used primarily in fish cookery to override the strong odor of certain types of fish.

toddy alcoholic beverage made from palm juice.

toor (toorvar) dal split yellow lentil; see *arhar dal,* this Guide.

tori ridged gourd; see *ghosala*.

tulsi Indian or holy basil (*Ocimum canum*), a variety of basil used to make herbal drinks. The plant is considered sacred and is used in certain Hindu religious ceremonies.

ubla anda boiled egg.

urad (urd) dal black gram, a lentil named for its black seed coat. The lentil without its seed coat is cream-colored, usually split, and known then as white gram. Relative to other lentils, this type takes much longer to cook. It usually is soaked, and often ground, before cooking. The lentil undergoes natural fermentation, which imparts a characteristic flavor to several classic southern Indian dishes. See *appam, idli, dosai* and *vada* in the *Menu Guide*.

val dal split lablab bean (*Dolichos lablab*), a whitish-yellow lentil.

vanaspati ghee vegetable shortening.

varq (warq) paper-thin, edible silver (silver leaf) or gold foil (gold leaf) used for decoration of sweets and meat dishes. The specific name for gold foil is *sone ka warq* (*varq*); for silver foil it is *chandi ka warq* (*varq*).

vilayati saunf aniseed.

vindaloo classic hot-and-sour curry with vinegar, a specialty of Goa.

yakhni meat broth.

zaafraan saffron; see *kesar*.

zamikand (jamikand) elephant-foot yam (*Amorphophallus campanulatus*); also called *suran*.

Bibliography

Achaya, K.T. *A Historical Dictionary of Indian Food*. Delhi: Oxford University Press, 1998.

Achaya, K.T. *Indian Food: A Historical Companion*. Delhi: Oxford University Press, 1998.

Agarwal, D.P. *The Archaeology of India*. New Delhi: Selectbook Service Syndicate, 1984.

Allchin, Bridget and Raymond. *The Rise of Civilization in India and Pakistan*. Cambridge: Cambridge University Press, 1982.

Banerji, Chitrita. *Life and Food in Bengal*. New Delhi: Rupa & Co., 1993.

Bhatnagar, Sangeeta and R.K. Saxena. *Dastarkhwan-e-Awadh*. New Delhi: HarperCollins Publishers India, 1997.

Bravo da Costa Rodrigues, Maria de Lourdes. *Tasty Morsels: Goan Food Ingredients and Preparation*. Goa, India: L & L Publications.

Burton, David. *The Raj at Table: A Culinary History of the British in India*. New Delhi: Rupa & Co., 1995.

Chandra, Smita and Sanjeev Chandra. *Cuisines of India: The Art and Tradition of Regional Indian Cooking*. New York: HarperCollins Publishers, 2001.

Dar, Krishna Prasad. *Kashmiri Cooking*. London: Penguin Books, 1997.

Devi, Yamuna. *The Art of Indian Vegetarian Cooking: Lord Krishna's Cuisine*. New York: E.P. Dutton, 1999.

Fairservis, Walter A., Jr. *The Roots of Ancient India: The Archaeology of Early Indian Civilization,* 2nd edition, revised. Chicago: The University of Chicago Press, 1975.

Husain, Shehzad. *The Indian Cookbook*. London: Lorenz Books, 2002.

Hyma, Albert. *A History of the Dutch in the Far East*. Ann Arbor, Michigan: George Wahr Publishing Co., 1953.

Jaffrey, Madhur. *A Taste of India*. New York: Atheneum, 1986.

Kaimal, Maya. *Savoring the Spice Coast of India: Fresh Flavors from Kerala*. New York: HarperCollins Publishers, 2000.

Kalra, J. Inder Singh (Jiggs) and Pradeep Das Gupta. *Prasad: Cooking with Indian Masters*. New Delhi: Allied Publishers Limited, 2000.

Kalra, J. Inder Singh (Jiggs) and Pushpesh Pant. *Daawat*. New Delhi: Allied Publishers Limited, 2001.

Keay, John. *India: A History*. London: HarperCollins Publishers, 2000.

Kenoyer, Jonathan Mark, editor. *Old Problems and New Perspectives in the Archaeology of South Asia*. Wisconsin Archaeological Reports, Volume 2. Madison, Wisconsin: University of Wisconsin Department of Anthropology, 1989.

Koshy, M.O. *The Dutch Power in Kerala (1729–1758)*. New Delhi, India: Mittal Publications, 1989.

Marks, Copeland. *The Varied Kitchens of India: Cuisines of the Anglo-Indians of Calcutta, Bengalis, Jews of Calcutta, Kashmiris, Parsis, and Tibetans of Darjeeling*. New York: M. Evans and Company, Inc., 1986.

Mathew, K.M. *Kerala Cookery*. Kerala, India: K.M. Mathew, 1999.

Panjabi, Camellia. *The Great Curries of India*. New York: Simon & Schuster, 1995.

Poonen, T.I. *A Survey of the Rise of the Dutch Power in Malabar (1603–78)*. Trichinopoly, India: St. Joseph's Industrial School Press, 1948.

Possehl, Gregory L. *Indus Age: The Beginnings*. Philadelphia, Pennsylvania: University of Pennsylvania Press, 1999.

Prakash, Om. *The Dutch East India Company and the Economy of Bengal, 1630–1720*. Princeton, New Jersey: Princeton University Press, 1985.

Prakash, Om. *Food and Drinks in Ancient India: From Earliest Times to c. 1200 A.D.* Delhi: Munshi Ram Manohar Lal, 1961.

Pruthi, J.S. *India—The Land and the People: Spices and Condiments*, 5th edition. New Delhi: National Book Trust, 1998.

Rau, Santha Rama. *The Cooking of India*. New York: Time-Life Books, 1975.

Ray, Sumana. *Indian Regional Cooking*. Secaucus, New Jersey: Chartwell Books, Inc., 1986.

Reejhsinghani, Arooni. *Best of Indian Sweets and Desserts*. Mumbai, India: Jaico Publishing House, 2001.

Sahni, Julie. *Classic Indian Cooking*. New York: William Morrow and Company, Inc., 1980.

Sengupta, Padmini. *Everday Life in Ancient India,* 2nd edition. London: Oxford University Press, 1957.

Singh, Digvijaya. *Cooking Delights of the Maharajas: Exotic Dishes from the Princely House of Sailana*. Mumbai, India: Vakils, Feffer & Simons Ltd., 1998.

Tammita-Delgoda, Sinharaja. *A Traveller's History of India,* 2nd edition. New York: Interlink Books, 1999.

Vairavan, Alamelu and Patricia Marquardt. *The Art of South Indian Cooking*. New York: Hippocrene Books, 1997.

Winius, George D. and Marcus P.M. Vink. *The Merchant-Warrior Pacified: The VOC (The Dutch East India Company) and its Changing Political Economy in India*. Delhi, India: Oxford University Press, 1991.

Index